Stirred NOT SHAKEN

Stirred NOT SHAKEN

THEMES *for an* EMERGING GENERATION

MARK FELDMEIR

CHALICE PRESS
ST. LOUIS, MISSOURI

© Copyright 2005 by Mark Feldmeir

All rights reserved. For permission to reuse content, please contact Copyright Clearance Center, 222 Rosewood Drive, Danvers, MA 01923, (978) 750-8400, www.thenewcopyright.com.

Biblical quotations, unless otherwise noted, are from the *New Revised Standard Version Bible*, copyright 1989, Division of Christian Education of the National Council of the Churches of Christ in the United States of America. Used by permission. All rights reserved.

Cover and interior design: Elizabeth Wright

This book is printed on acid-free, recycled paper.

Visit Chalice Press on the World Wide Web at
www.chalicepress.com

10 9 8 7 6 5 4 3 2 1   05 06 07 08 09

Library of Congress Cataloging-in-Publication Data

Feldmeir, Mark R.
  Stirred, not shaken : themes for an emerging generation / Mark R. Feldmeir.
    p. cm.
  ISBN 13: 978-0-827234-59-7 (pbk. : alk. paper)
  ISBN 10: 0-827234-59-7
  1. United Methodist Church (U.S.)—Sermons. 2. Sermons, American—21st century. I. Title.
  BX8333.F357S75 2005
  252'.076—dc22

2004014436

Printed in the United States of America

Contents

Introduction	1
Part 1: Ambiguity	7
As If It Were So—1 Samuel 17	11
The Splintered Throne—Mark 10:32–45	18
The Journey of the Magi—Matthew 2:1–12	23
Every Here and Now—Isaiah 40:21–31	30
You Have No Idea—Mark 9:2–9	37
Part 2: Suffering	45
All That You Can't Leave Behind—Mark 8:31–38	47
The Time of Your Life—John 12:20–33	53
Blessed Thorns—2 Corinthians 12:2–10	60
The Big Reveal—Luke 24:36–48	67
It Takes One to Know One—1 Corinthians 1:18–25	73
Part 3: Transformation	79
Home Alone—Luke 2:41–52	81
Keepers of the Flame—Matthew 25:1–13	87
Born to Run—Hebrews 12:1–2	93
One Life to Give—Mark 12:38–44	101
Get Up and Walk—John 5:1–9	108

Part: 4 Reconciliation　　　　　　　　　　　　　　　　115

　　Road Work Ahead—Luke 3:1–6　　　　　　　117

　　Vision Quest—Mark 10:46–52　　　　　　　　124

　　Trading Places—Luke 1:47–55　　　　　　　　131

　　Signed, Sealed, Delivered—Mark 1:9–13　　　138

Notes　　　　　　　　　　　　　　　　　　　　　147

Introduction

Esquire recently published a small book curiously titled, *What It Feels Like,* in which more than fifty true, first-person accounts of some of life's most exhilarating, harrowing, and bizarre experiences are described in very colorful detail. If you have ever wondered what it feels like to walk on the moon, or to be attacked by a grizzly bear, or to have a parachute fail, or suffer from narcolepsy or the Ebola virus, then you will no doubt be entertained and informed by this provocative collection. It presupposes that ours is a generation with a serious appetite for the peculiar, the unknown, and the real; and it points to the fact that we are a generation that possesses a deep appreciation for the first-person narrative. Sharing our experience is far more compelling than communicating what we think or know, or the answers we supply—regardless of how genuine those answers may be. In our culture, the one with the best story tends to draw the largest audience. And I believe this is good news for those of us who preach these days.

When preachers sit down to prepare sermons for their congregations, they would do well to ask the question early on in the creative process— *"What does it feel like?"* What does it feel like to walk around inside this particular biblical story? What does it feel like to follow Christ in a post-Christian culture? What does it feel like to live in this particular community, in this particular part of the world, at this particular time? What does it feel like to be twenty-three, or eighty-eight, or head-over-heels in love, or terminally ill? Preachers who ask such questions before they set pen to paper will often hear their people comment later, "You must have been reading my mind this morning," or, "You seemed to be speaking directly to me." But I also believe the preacher will hear a word from God too before the sermon has even been prepared and preached—a word that affirms that *the Word became flesh and lived among us, and we have seen his glory.*

Incarnational preaching must be contextual preaching, and the real challenge every preacher faces is to be faithful to the particular context of his or her community so that the Word might dwell most fully within it. This is not to be confused, however, with so-called "relevant" preaching, which often serves only to confirm what our listeners already know or expect to hear, and reduces the Bible to manageable "principles" or "keys" for *improving* our lives rather than *transforming* them. Such preaching tends to offer prescriptions for *surviving* or *succeeding* in this world rather than offering a description of life lived in the kingdom of God, which demands nothing less than our full *conversion.*

The kind of preaching I am advocating acknowledges where the people are, but does not allow them to stay there for very long, inviting them instead to see the kingdom of God and to pledge their citizenship there. It begins with stories and images of real life and human experience, and seeks to address that context with what we understand to be the life and experience of God. That is a dangerous thing to do, of course, given the fact that we are operating on such limited information.

Who are the people to whom we preach? What are their questions, their struggles, their doubts, their joys? What are the channels of communication with which they are accustomed? How will we shape the Word—through images, through story, through doctrine, through the artistic and cultural expressions of our particular contexts? This is not a new method, by the way. In relating the kingdom of God to the people of his day, Jesus put a child on his lap, or pointed to a fig tree, or held in his fingers a single mustard seed, or broke an ordinary loaf of bread. Jesus seemed always to know his sheep, and he met them in their own world.

I preach in a very particular context, which requires of me a very particular word. I begin with particularity, trusting that whatever I preach to the people of my congregation will have at least a thread of truth for those outside of it. Because I love and live among the people of my congregation, I know that I am speaking *for* them, not simply to them, and I also know that whatever I preach must be true for me if my listeners will find any truth in it for themselves.

My particular listeners are predominately, though not exclusively, young people between the ages of twenty-five and forty-five. They are overworked, overstretched, well-educated, and in constant transition with their families, their parents, their careers, and their responsibilities and roles. They are high achievers, fairly good-looking, generally rich by worldly standards, and at least slightly above average. They are also searching for meaning, community, purpose, relationships, security, six-pack abs, buns of steel, and a faith that intersects with the tangible realities of their lives.

As I have dwelled among them for the last ten years I have come to understand a few things about them that have influenced my preaching in their context. These themes are not unique to their experience, or necessarily to their generation. In fact, in many ways they reflect in more general terms the changing landscape of the culture in which we all do ministry.

First, they live daily in the land of *ambiguity*. Things are not always what they seem in their lives, and their faith is replete with the experience of irony. They often have as many doubts as answers, and seek a context in which their doubts can be honestly shared. They prefer to wrestle with their faith rather than having it spoon-fed to them by one in authority, and they often admit that Jesus rarely seems to make much rational sense. They are deeply suspicious of institutions—particularly religious institutions—and are more interested in becoming part of a movement rather than joining a religion. When they come to church, they do not seek maps of certainty in order to find their way to God; instead, they seek a sense of direction, and the freedom to find their own cadence on their journey.

Second, they are inspired and emboldened by the *suffering* of Jesus Christ, through which they can begin to make sense of their own suffering, and by which they are motivated to offer themselves to the world more freely. They do not tend to view the suffering and death of Jesus *solely* through the lens of a theology of atonement. They believe that the suffering and self-offering of Jesus makes Jesus more human, which in turn gives their own suffering deep spiritual meaning, and provides a central model for the giving of oneself to the deep needs and hurts of the world. For them, the cross is a primary symbol of God's solidarity with those who suffer and a sign that points to our shared Christian vocation of self-offering and sacrifice.

Third, seeking an alternative to the constant and seductive lure of cultural conformity, personal *transformation* is central to their experience of God. They demand a holy word from God about real life, the time of their lives, the problems of the world, and the signs of God's presence in their own little corner of the world. They seek ways to sacramentalize their world—making holy the simple, ordinary stuff of their daily lives, such as family, work, recreation, money, relationships, and the environment. They reject the modern dualism of body and soul, matter and spirit, church and world, and they seek ways to affirm the whole self as a holy means of grace. Belonging to a deeply pragmatic generation, they want their lives to count for something, and they want to make a difference in the world.

And fourth, they hunger for *reconciliation*—in their personal relationships, in the world, and in the household of God. They understand that they cannot love God and hate another, yet there is a profound relational tension all around them. They know the burden of broken families—as both children and adults; they know that Christians are deeply divided over the same issues that divide society; and they know, too, the cavernous divisions in their own relationships—with God, with each other, with their own selves. This tension is met with a deep hunger for community, for a relationship with God that claims and names them, for a distinctive confession of faith that sets them apart without alienating them from others.

These are the particular people who fill the seats of my church on Sunday mornings, and I suspect that they are not strangers to your church. They represent the current emerging generation of Christians and seekers in North America, though word has it that fewer of them are attending our churches these days. This is no secret, and plenty has been written on how to find them, market them, and reel them in—all of which, I believe, is part of the problem.

While I do not pretend to know the answer, I trust that at least part of it lies in our ability as preachers to maintain an honest contextual focus in our preaching, and to dare to stand within that context as a member of their community. From that place, tell them *what it feels like*—to walk in the story as *you* walk in the story, to live in the world that *you* live in, to struggle with the same doubts and questions with which *you* struggle, to know the grace of Christ that *you* have known, and to be stirred, not shaken, in a world in which every foundation seems to be shaking and splitting all around us.

Readers of this collection will note my frequent use of film clips from major motion pictures. Most of the sermons include suggestions for thematically relevant film clips, many of which have been woven into the body of the sermon and can be projected on a screen during the preaching event. (A church *must* have a license or obtain permission to do this legally and ethically. The Christian Video Licensing International Web site [www.cvli.org] has information about such licenses; annual fees are based on worship attendance.) In some cases, I offer an alternative suggestion for preachers who may choose to take a slightly different approach to the sermon theme.

The use of film clips in worship is not the normative means of communication in most congregations, nor is it a necessary one. Some will argue that the skilled preacher can do without them, while others will argue that the use of film clips communicates a depth of cultural engagement and an entryway to the gospel that invites the listeners to see and experience the grace of God in the images and stories with which they are familiar. I suggest that the faithful and effective use of film clips should follow three simple rules:

1. *Keep it theological.* Does the clip illustrate the gospel of Jesus Christ? Does it name the spiritual, relational, and collective struggles of our generation? Does it carry the doctrinal theme of the sermon in a manner that is consistent with the common experience of God in the context of your congregation? Does it subvert or confront the cultural gospel, which idolizes individualism, greed, competition, the "power of the human spirit" (a common cinematic device), and the myth of personal autonomy? To put it more simply, the clip must serve as a window through which we can see an aspect of the kingdom of God and/or the brokenness of humanity, rather than simply providing a mere reflection of our own sense of goodness, moral authority, and self-sufficiency.

2. *Keep it brief.* Our listeners do not come to worship to see a movie, but to hear a word from God. I suggest using clips that are no more than three or four minutes in length, and which require minimal introduction. If you have to explain the "point" of the clip after it has been viewed, the clip most likely did not serve its proper purpose in the sermon.

3. *Keep it seamless.* Ensure that your multimedia team is prepared to play the clip at the appropriate time in the sermon. Avoid awkward delays in the delivery; rehearse with your team, if necessary; and be attentive to language in the clip that may distract or offend your listeners. Honor the sacred time and space of worship, as well as the ethos of your congregation.

The sermons in this collection have been arranged thematically, according to the themes I have mentioned above. They were preached over the last year among the people at Santa Margarita United Methodist Church, whom I have loved and with whom I have lived for the last ten years. I am grateful for their trust, their encouragement, and their innovative spirit.

In addition, I want to thank Cal and Ann Shores for providing me a place to retreat and complete this project; the late Jane McAvoy at Chalice Press for her encouragement and direction; and my wife, Lori, and my three children—Alyson, Casey, and Matthew—who remind me daily *what it feels like* to love and be loved.

Mark R. Feldmeir

PART 1

Ambiguity

One week before Christmas, on the fourth Sunday of Advent, the Chancel Choir performed a Christmas cantata that told the story of the Advent of Christ, including the prophet Isaiah declaring Israel's coming redemption, the prophet John proclaiming a baptism for the forgiveness of sins, and the angel Gabriel announcing to Mary that the Lord was with her. Gabriel's good news came in the form of a solo, performed by a member of the church who was in the midst of one of the most painful seasons of his life. He had lost his job nine months prior, one of four million other Americans who did not survive the abrupt downsizing of corporate America over the last few years. While waiting for job interviews that never materialized, he answered daily phone calls from collection agencies, burned through the last of his savings, lived off of beans and weenies on a meager unemployment check, and held off the mortgage company which threatened foreclosure on his modest home. By December his situation looked bleak, and there was no end in sight. And yet there he stood before the congregation, as if he had been appointed by God to deliver the one word that could be delivered by none other on that day, and that few of us could understand as well as him. *"Be not afraid,"* he sang above the heads of the choir. *"Be not afraid, for you have found favor with God."* Some might have called that irony, but those of us who gathered there that morning called it testimony.

There was a time in North America in which the preacher could assume a stable and broad theological consensus among the listening community, as well as a dependable degree of receptivity and authority within the broader cultural context. The pre-Enlightenment, pre-modern preacher could assume a consciousness among the listening community that could not imagine a world without God, without the Church, without an established, assumed "truth." The modern, Enlightenment preacher, while seriously challenged by the emergence of a thinking autonomy in the world, maintained a central place in public life by appealing to a "civic faith," which affirmed that belief in God is largely a private matter, though useful to the public realm insofar as it legitimizes and serves the values and agendas of those in power.

Many of the listeners in our congregations, and many mainline preachers, assume that the modern context still exists in twenty-first century North America. To some extent it does; however, many Christians have sensed an increasing cultural hostility or a palpable apathy toward the gospel, the church, the preacher, and God. Preachers no longer occupy a place of privilege and authority from which we can simply call our listeners to assent to a set of beliefs and faith claims. Our message is held under deep suspicion, perceived by many who remain outside the church to be neither intellectually credible nor socially acceptable in a culture that prizes autonomy, success, competition, and self-sufficiency.[1]

It is one thing for the preacher to stand before the congregation and croon the daring words of Gabriel, "Be not afraid," from a position of power and certainty, perhaps even offering proven principles for conquering fear and solving one's particular problems. But it is quite another to hear from one who knows something of what it means to face real fear, deep loss, and the ambiguity of a faith that does not presume to know how the story will end ahead of time. The credibility of our message is grounded in the honest acknowledgment of that experience of ambiguity, where old answers are challenged by new, concrete struggles; where the promises of the Canon are faithfully held in tension by the realities of our particular experience; where our rational consciousness meets an unpredictable God, creating a kind of crisis in which faith becomes risky and dangerous, irrational and reckless.

The sermons in this first unit address some of the big issues of life and the complexities and ambiguities of living faithfully in the world. For the emerging generation of Christians and seekers, easy answers that seek to resolve our common struggles are not adequate. Our listeners have a deep suspicion that life is as messy and unpredictable for the biblical characters as it is for us today. In the following sermons, a young David calls us to a kind of faith that makes risk a necessity; Jesus subverts our claim to glory, offering in its place a life of sacrifice; the magi remind us that not all well-planned journeys lead straight to God; Isaiah points us to the unmistakable presence of God, which is often concealed by circumstance, yet revealed from the very beginning of time; and the disciples remind us that faith is trust in the absence of the facts.

In the midst of such ambiguity and uncertainty, we stand *among* our people, offering a fragile testimony, a contested word, an honest utterance—*"Be not afraid, for you have found favor with God."*

As If It Were So

1 Samuel 17

"Let no one's heart fail God because of this giant. I will go and fight the Philistine."

I will never forget Paul Reece.[1] I was a sophomore in high school, fifteen years old, 5'5" and about 138 pounds soaking wet. Paul Reece was also a sophomore, but to me it seemed as if he was about thirty-two years old, measuring 6'4" and weighing in at around 280 pounds. We both played on the JV football team. Actually, Paul Reece played on the football team; most of the time, I watched from the sidelines. Paul Reece was the consummate football player—big and hairy, with the added quality of being cruel. I, on the other hand, was a cross-country runner in full pads. I never should have even played football in high school. I confess openly that it was not one of the more brilliant moves of my young life.

Paul Reece helped me see the light on that issue. Before the season started, in the blistering heat of an August afternoon, the coach set up tackling drills. One group went twenty yards down field—this was the ball-carrier group. The other group stayed put—this was the tackling group. Each player in the group downfield had a simple task. Carry the ball and run at the tackler without trying to avoid him. Just run at him. Hard. Bury your head, plow forward, and stay on your feet. The tackler, from what I could tell, also had a simple task. Don't die. Pray. Tell God you're sorry for everything. Bargain with him. Pray that the ball carrier will have mercy, or that he'll trip, or that he's at least smaller than you—which on this team, given my stature, was not very likely.

So the coach divides us up. I'm a tackler. I'm fifth in line. Being one of the only players on the team who can count, I look down field, count five back from the front, and that's my guy, right? I remember counting—1, 2, 3, 4…and *Lord have mercy*. Paul Reece is number five in line. He sees me gaping at him. He waves at me. I see him talking to the guys around him. They are all laughing, scheming, planning my imminent death. He's shaking his legs out like a boxer in the ring, knocking his oversized head back and forth to loosen it up. Meanwhile, I'm looking for an opening in the fence and wondering how far I could run before the coach would catch me.

Did I happen to say that playing high school football was not one of my most brilliant moves in life?

The coach blew the whistle once. That was your signal to step up to the line and take your mark. By then it was surreal. I felt like I was already being pulled to the light, you know? When the coach blew the whistle again, it sounded like "Taps" on a bugle. I don't remember a whole lot after that second whistle, to tell you the truth. I remember the image of Paul Reece's fat freckled doughboy face stuffed tightly in his blue helmet; I remember the drool dripping from the corners of his mouth; I remember the sound of feet, that horrible sound of a stampede; the grunting, animal sounds he made, and the sound of that cataclysmic collision—like a car crash on the 405 Freeway.

I do not remember flying. This was the only time in my life that I actually took flight, and I do not remember it. I do not remember how my helmet was completely turned around on my head. I do not remember the quiet hush of coaches and teammates looking down at me, nor do I remember how long I was down. I only remember the coach standing over me, looking down, adjusting my helmet, grabbing the face mask, shaking it, and shouting over and over again, "*Feldman, are you okay? Feldman, get up.*" And I also remember looking around, and seeing Paul Reece down on one knee, shaking his head, trying to shake it off.

I lost the battle that day. Paul Reece scrambled my eggs, and my coach didn't even know my last name. My body had been pummeled. My left shoulder still cracks and crunches and reminds me of Paul Reece every day, twenty years later. But even in defeat, I gained a crucial victory in my life. Paul Reece didn't scare me anymore. Paul

Reece was just a big, fat kid with red hair whose gene pool was under-chlorinated. After that experience, I could look at him, and he could look at me, and there was a quiet understanding. He gave me his best shot, and I got up. I took the best shot from the biggest freak on the team, and I survived.

Not all battles end in victory, but in every one of life's battles, insofar as we live to tell about it later, there is a victory: I'm still here; it didn't kill me. Yes, I paid the price, had my bell rung, but I survived. And I can look at that thing now—that thing I was so afraid of, that thing that growled at me every time I looked at it. I can look at it now, and it doesn't scare me, because I now know that it can't get to the stuff that only God has access to—that stuff made not of physical power and might, but of Spirit.

David had been there. David had dwelled in the land of giants and lived to tell about every one of them. And when the biggest, meanest giant of them all showed up on the battlefield one day, David remembered.

You have heard the story. King Saul had already sold out. He had grown desperate, for there was no one in all of Israel who dared to face the great giant, not even the great king himself. But word comes to him about some radical out in the fields talking with the troops, some idealist who still believes passionately in the dream of "God and Country." So Saul calls this character into his office, only to discover that he's just a kid who's probably spent too much time in the sun tending his father's sheep. David pleads his case, "I can take care of this giant once and for all," he declares. But Saul is unconvinced. He knows that this would be a bad political move; the press would tear him apart if he threw a young lad into the ring against the giant. No way. But David is too headstrong; he pleads passionately, but Saul says *no*. He speaks of dreams and ideals and bravery and hope, but still, the answer is *no*. And then David finally lets fall from his lips the one word that causes Saul to grow intensely still: "Yahweh," says David. "The great Yahweh, the God who delivered Israel from Egypt, the God who delivered Israel from oppression and destruction time and time again, the God who made you king of this nation, this God will also deliver me from the Philistines. I know, because he's delivered me before, when I've been out in the fields wrestling lions and bears to save the sheep. He's delivered me, and he'll deliver me again," David says. And now Saul is moved. The speech, the faith, the vision, the conviction—it's all very compelling. "Go," he says, "and may Yahweh be with you."

And then the dramatic story looks more like comedy. Saul dresses David in his own armor and begins to walk him to the door. But David can't move under the weight of all that armor; the coat is too bulky, the helmet keeps slipping over his eyes, and the sword is just too heavy. So David, without giving it a second thought, takes off the armor, pulls out a sling, loads his shepherd's bag with five smooth stones, and heads out the door to meet the nasty giant called Goliath. The next part of the story amounts to nothing more than a little pre-fight mudslinging. But when all the trash talk is said and done and the bell finally rings, David casts his single stone, and you can still hear the violent thud of a huge Philistine warrior as his face crashes against the hardened soil of the battlefield.

It's been said that faith is believing in spite of the evidence, and watching the evidence change. In David's case, the evidence was overwhelming—a big, hairy, audacious giant with a serious attitude and an undefeated record, challenging an entire nation to hit him with their best shot. Not a single soul would dare rise to the occasion; Israel's armies scattered in fear. It looked like the entire nation would be toasted and buttered by the Philistines. But David—fresh from the fields of sheepherding and songwriting—spoke the one word of faith that proved more courageous than the actual deed that would later bring the giant down. Standing in front of the king and his armies, David proclaimed, "Let no one's heart fail God because of this giant. I will go and fight the Philistine."

Some people laughed. Others doubted. But a few were filled with hope, because David pointed to God when most people could only see giants in their eyes. What David was saying, of course, is that either God is, or God isn't. What we say and believe about God is either true completely—that God is indeed a mighty deliverer, quick to save, worthy of our faith and trust—or it isn't true at all. And David was saying that he, despite being the most unlikely candidate for giant-slaying, was willing to act as if it were so, as if it were true, as if God would deliver, as if what he believed actually mattered.

What brought Goliath down was not merely a smooth river stone slung from David's sling. What brought Goliath down was a faith that was determined, at all costs, to not fail God's heart with hopelessness and despair, but to cling to God as if God mattered, as if everything he had known about God was so and true.

For David, failure, even to the point of defeat, was not the thing that disappoints God. The way David saw it, hopelessness and despair were the things that fail God—the excuses for why we can't act, why we can't try, why we can't consider doing something that is seemingly impossible according to the world's standards. David had plenty of excuses at hand. He was the most unlikely candidate, the least of Jesse's children, the fairest, most fragile—stuck out in the fields with the sheep because he was not equipped physically for fighting. But David had something the rest seemed to lack. David had a kind of courage born of God—a courage no giant in this world could conquer.

There comes a time in life for all of us when, if we are to act as if the promises of God are true, we must realize that we do not have to be qualified to do what must be done. There comes a time when we just have to go ahead and do it, even though we are not convinced that we can do it as well as we think it ought to be done. This is the distinguishing feature of a person of faith. It is what makes believers out of kings and heroes out of shepherds. And it will either bring down the giants before us or, in the event that those giants get the best of us, it will turn our failure into a sacrament—a means of grace by which God raises us up again.

Sometimes all we can see are the giants in our midst—the terrifying diagnosis for which we are completely unprepared; the debilitating regrets that keep us stuck in the past; the mountains of problems that keep us stuck in the present; the sin, the fear, the shortcomings, and the weaknesses. We see those giants and we say, "That story about David makes for a great Sunday school lesson, but let's be real—I am not David." But I want you to look at this David. This is not King David; this is not the Warrior David who killed his ten-thousands; this is not the David to whom God would promise an eternal dynasty. That part of David's history had not yet been written. This David is a mere shepherd boy—young, ruddy, and handsome. No combat qualifications, no convincing resume, no reputation.

But David did not permit the giant problem of today to eclipse the promises of a God who had a history. David listened to his life.

He listened to where God was, where God had been, and what he heard was the story of a God who delivered him time and again from the bears and lions, and this was the same God who would deliver all of Israel from the Philistines. David had seen enough in his own life to be convinced that what God says is what God does. And he knew that there was nothing that could separate him from that promise, from that story, from the very heart of God. David would rather fail trying to prove his faith in God than fail God by trying to preserve a future without him.

That doesn't mean that David did not have his doubts. It simply means that his doubts did not define him. Paul Tillich defined faith as courage. Tillich said that when you examine a life of faith, it will look a lot like courage, and such courage will not remove doubts, but transcend them.

We are apt to think that the opposite of faith is doubt. We think that if we have doubts we don't have faith. But faith does not remove doubt. Faith is courage to face the unknown in spite of our doubts. Our knees will still tremble; the lump in the throat will be palpable; disappointment and defeat will still be a very real possibility. But the measure of our faith is determined by the distance we are willing to go into the unknowns of life, trusting that the promises of God are either true completely in the here and now, or not true at all.

That is why the apostle Paul could be so bold when he spoke of the love of God. Paul had seen it all—shipwrecks, imprisonment, beatings, hunger, persecution. You name the giant—Paul had seen it all. And what does he say?

> What then are we to say about these things? If God is for us, who is against us?...Who will separate us from the love of Christ? Will hardship, or distress, or persecution, or famine, or nakedness, or peril, or sword?...No, in all these things we are more than conquerors through him who loved us. For I am convinced that neither death, nor life, nor angels, nor rulers, nor things present, nor things to come, nor powers, nor height, nor depth, nor anything else in all creation, will be able to separate us from the love of God in Christ Jesus our Lord. (Rom. 8:31, 35, 37–39)

What made David courageous before men was not that he felled a giant Philistine. That was not the courageous deed. That was just a consequence of a far greater courageous act—the act of calling on God, Yahweh, and remembering God's faithfulness—of naming it, proclaiming it, trusting it, calling on it, and finally acting on it. That was what made David a courageous man and a brilliant leader. That is what made him a man after God's own heart.

Young William Wilberforce was discouraged one night in the early 1790s after another defeat in his ten-year battle against the slave trade in England. Tired and frustrated, he opened his Bible and began to leaf through it. A small piece of paper fell out and fluttered to the floor. It was a letter written by John Wesley shortly before his death. Wilberforce read it again: "Unless the divine power has raised you up...I see not how you can go through your glorious enterprise in opposing that [abominable practice of slavery), which is the scandal of religion, of England, and of human nature. Unless God has raised you up for this very thing, you will be worn out by the opposition of men and devils. But if God be for you, who can be against you? Are all of them together stronger than God? Oh, be not weary of well-doing. Go on in the name of God, and in the power of His might."[2]

There are giants in every life, and battles waged both within and without—some of which we have endured for what seems like a lifetime, some of which will come and go with the seasons of our lives, but none of which will end in defeat for the one who dares to enter the battlefield armed with the sacred memory of God's faithfulness.

The first act of courage in the face of every giant is not a matter of doing, but of remembering. The next is to proceed as if it were so and true. The rest is none of our business.

Video Clip Suggestion

Indiana Jones and the Last Crusade (Paramount Pictures, 1989)
(To illustrate the inherent risk in faith and life)
On a quest for the coveted Grail, Indy takes the biggest risk of his life in order to save the life of his father: He must cross the invisible bridge and trust that he will make it across (1:45:35—1:48:57).

The Splintered Throne

Mark 10:32–45

"Are you able to drink the cup that I drink?" (Mk. 10:38)

After visiting Washington, D.C., a couple of weeks ago, I am convinced that there is a monument for everybody who has ever been a somebody. It is different here in California. Do something big out here, make a name for yourself, and you get a little star on Hollywood Blvd. next to a sewer grate and a pawn shop. If you are a real star, perhaps someone will cast your likeness in wax and stick you in a museum with other almost-famous dead people, right? But in D.C., you've got to be bigger than big, right? They use limestone and bronze instead of wax for important people, and they enshrine them in domes and surround them with hand-hewn pillars of stone. It is so dramatic. Stand in front of Lincoln as he sits perched on his throne, and you can almost hear his heart beat for freedom, and feel his heart break over the blood-stained soil at Gettysburg. Stand before Jefferson's timeless pose and you can see in his eyes his daring vision of democracy and his unfettered hope for humankind. Sit down on the bench next to F.D.R., and you can still hear his sound-bite preaching on the evils of war and his compassion for the poor and destitute. You spend enough time in D.C. and you start to wonder what in the world you're doing with *your* life, and how in this world *you* will be remembered, if at all.

So I'm sitting on a bench eating a hot dog in front of the White House, thinking about greatness—what it takes, what it looks like, how to find it—when a stranger passing on the sidewalk says to me, "Hey buddy, can I have a swig of your Coke?" I think he was John the Baptist—you know, he had fire in his eyes and the sour smell of the city filling his airspace and teeth like a wind-beaten pirate; he was a prophet of God, sent to tell the truth on me. Here I am reflecting on greatness, right? I'm thinking to myself, "I'm thirty-five now. It's time to make my mark in this world, time to do something great, something big, make history, suffer for humanity, write a speech to change the world, give my life for a great cause, open a vein and bleed heroically, get fitted for the limestone memorial"—and God just wants a swig of my Coke. I watched him raise the bottle to his cracked lips, tip his head back, and take a long, hard swallow. When he came up for air, he tried to give the bottle back to me, with a knowing smile, but I insisted that he keep it. My thoughts, after all, were set on greatness.

I am not alone. James and John had greatness on their minds, too, and they didn't get it either. On the road to Jerusalem, Jesus is telling them what they are too thick-headed to hear. The Son of God will be arrested, mocked, spat on, convicted of crimes he did not commit, and killed. It's the third time he's told them this, and the third time they've failed to hear it. They are too blind to see. Mark says Jesus tells them three times. Before he tells them of his fate the first time, Jesus heals a blind man. After he tells them a third time, Jesus immediately heals another blind man. You get what Mark is doing here? The blind can see who Jesus really is, but those with sight are still blind. He's talking about the cross the whole time, but they're thinking about thrones.

Maybe that says something about the power of denial; maybe it says something about the seductive illusion of success and glory. Jesus was a *somebody*. His disciples were somebodies because of him. All the healings, the dramatic exorcisms, the miracles—they all pointed to greatness, to a throne, to power, to a new political administration in Israel. Jesus was the Messiah, and messiahs do not die. Messiahs can't be dead if they're going to save the nation—it's just not an option. In their minds, Jesus was traveling to Jerusalem not to die on a cross but to ascend the throne, which is why James and John interrupt the conversation about the cross and the suffering. "Jesus," they say, "about that throne. Do you think, after the election, when you make your cabinet appointments—do you think you could put the two of us right up there at the top with you?"

Are you able to drink the cup that I drink, he asks? But they are not the sharpest knives in the drawer. The poetry is lost on them. "Yes, Lord. We are able. Absolutely. Just tell us what you want us to do, and it's done. Just give us the cup of glory, and we'll knock it down right here."

That is part of our problem, isn't it? We have no idea what is in that cup that Jesus would have us drink from. No clue. We think it is the cup of glory, of victory, of blessing, right? Do something big, get blessed for it. *Give me the cup Jesus. I'll take one long drink from it and will not come up for air until the last drop drips on my tongue. One big drink—all at once. Bring it on. Just give me the cup and I'll show you.* And we raise that cup to our lips, and we find that it's not what we expected at all. We can't handle it. What is in that cup is bitter. We expected something more like Raspberry-Mango, but it's as sour as a lemon drop. We thought it was the cup of glory, but it turns out to be the cup of sacrifice. Every time we dare to drink of it, it sets our teeth on edge and makes the bottom of our feet itch. It burns going down. And we discover that, to follow Jesus, we've got to take little sips—little slow sips, over time, over a lifetime.

I do not know of any other way, really. I keep waiting for my big, Raspberry-Mango moment in life—every Christian does; every preacher does. When the bishop laid his hands on my head and ordained me, he said, *"Preach the good news. Make disciples. Baptize."* It all sounded so glorious at the time. Raspberry-Mango ministry. Become a pastor and people adore you, right? *Pastor this and Pastor that.* You're going to be so important. And twelve years later, here I am, still taking out the trash and scrubbing toilets and pulling paper jams out of the copy machine. Is this the cup? Jesus says that someone has to do it. Little sips, over time. It's a whole lifetime of little sips from that cup.

Jesus once said that those who are faithful in little are faithful in much, and God knows the little is enough to keep us busy for a lifetime. Jesus does the great flip-flop with our definition of greatness in this world. It turns out that greatness isn't a limestone monument or a star on the walk of fame. It is not aspiring toward some heroic deed that will make the headlines of the evening news or the history books of future generations. While the world cherishes its heroes, Jesus did not seem to make such distinctions between people. Kingdom living, according to Jesus, is far simpler than that, and far less self-concerned. For most of us, it will be, as Fred Craddock reminds us, a lifetime of taking little sips from that cup of self-offering that Jesus raises to our lips.¹ That is what makes the world turn; that is what brings the Kingdom into view for a world that cannot see it clearly.

While we are off looking for moments of greatness in this life, someone still has to take those little sips. Someone still has to sit through the dark night with the dying when no one else can stay awake. Someone still has to empty the bedpans for the sick, and rock to sleep the crying infants, and dry the tears of the mourning, and carry the trash out to the curbside, and wait up in worry for the kids who don't make it home before curfew. And that is not Raspberry-Mango ministry for any of us. But I will tell you this much: It it is the cup from which Jesus calls us to drink—the cup of self-giving, the cup of sacrifice that, when we drink from it, has a way of setting someone else free from their own suffering, which may be for them too much to bear.

James and John could not see it that way, and the truth is that most of us cannot see it that way either. It was expected that when the Messiah finally arrived, he would take away the world's suffering. Jesus said as much in Luke 4: the lame would walk, the oppressed would be set free, the blind would see, and the hungry bellies of the poor would be filled. "Sit tight," they said, "hang in there. The Messiah is on the way. I can't help you, but there is one who is coming who can." What they did not understand was that the Messiah, in raising the cup of suffering to his lips and drinking from it, would do something far more extraordinary than take away our suffering; he would share it with us, taking the suffering of the world on himself. Then he would pass the cup to those who dared still to go with him, saying, "Are you able?"

About a Boy is a wonderful film about a self-absorbed man, Will, whose life is transformed by a lonely, lost boy named Marcus, who seeks Will's companionship. In the movie Marcus has signed up for the school talent show, for which he has planned to sing his mother's favorite song, "Killing Me Softly," in front of the brutal, unforgiving audience of students. Will races to the show, but is unable to convince Marcus that singing "Killing Me Softly" will be, as he says, an act of social suicide. In a moment of courage and solidarity, Will emerges from backstage, bearing an electric guitar, and accompanies Marcus before a mocking crowd.

Jesus is on that stage, sharing the burden; giving himself in such a way that it frees someone else from the burden of drinking the bitter cup of life alone. Toni Morrison says that "the function of freedom is to free someone else," and that is what Jesus calls us to do with the freedom he gives us. "Can you drink the same cup from which I drink?" Little sips; few will understand; it won't get you a limestone memorial. But it will get you to the Kingdom.

Minnie Martin turned eighty-eight years old last week; yesterday morning, she joined the great company of the saints of heaven. As I sat with her this week, I saw a woman who had outlived two parents, two husbands, eight brothers and sisters, and just about every close friend she's ever had. I saw a woman who took little sips from that cup over the course of her entire life—caring for the sick, encouraging others, praying for people in need. I imagined the thousand skinned knees that she dressed, the ten thousand hands that she held, the million tears that she dried. It was a lifetime of little sips from the cup that Jesus gave her, and she held it with grace and courage for eighty-eight years.

In the ten years I had known Minnie Martin, I never once heard her pray, "Lord, I want you to do for me whatever I ask of you." Instead, she always seemed to be doing whatever the Lord asked of her, taking little sips every day of her life, until her cup was empty and she laid it down at last.

Video Clip Suggestions

The Princess Bride (Metro-Golwyn Mayer, 1987)

When the Princess commands "Farm Boy" to do countless acts of meaningless servitude, "Farm Boy" replies each time with the words, "as you wish," which, as the narrator says, is another way of saying "I love you" (0:02:25—0:03:27).

About a Boy (Universal Pictures, 2002)

Will races to the auditorium, walks out on stage with an electric guitar, and joins Marcus in singing "Killing Me Softly" at the school talent show before a crowd of mocking children (1:28:49—1:32:43).

The Journey of the Magi

Matthew 2:1–12

"Where is the child who has been born king of the Jews? For we observed his star at its rising, and have come to pay him homage." (Mt. 2:2)

Rancho Santa Margarita didn't appear on the map ten years ago. When the district superintendent called me in 1994 and asked me to consider an appointment to this new church, I immediately had stars in my eyes. She described it as a "wonderful opportunity with great potential and incredible possibilities—a perfect match for someone like me." I learned later that this is DS-speak for: "you are young and unproven and we have absolutely no idea where to send you." After our phone conversation I immediately checked my maps, but Rancho Santa Margarita did not appear on any of them. I called a few friends, who said, "Rancho *what?*" I went to the Automobile Club, and the woman behind the counter asked, "Are you sure that's in California?" She checked her computer, consulted with a co-worker, and finally pulled out a large map of South Orange County. With her yellow highlighter she carefully traced the journey, stopping abruptly where the road reached a dead end in Lake Forest. "This will get you close," she said. "How close?" I asked. "Within ten miles, I think."

Not every road we travel in life gets us to our destination. There are often ten miles of mystery to deal with, and nothing more than a single, sometimes faint, star hanging in the bleak sky, leading the way. And ours is a generation with a serious appetite for that unknown part of the journey. We set out in life, carrying in one hand the old maps passed down to us by our ancestors; and in the other, a bag of popcorn to mark the trails where the known road ends and the mystery begins.

We are not unfamiliar with the image of journey these days. We are, as they say, a generation of seekers and adventurers. We drive Expeditions™ and Land Rovers,™ Explorers™ and Highlanders,™ Hummers™ and Tahoes.™ We exchanged our ten speeds for mountain bikes, made the handheld GPS a household item, and mainstreamed extreme outdoor sports; we watch the Outdoor Life Network *(out you go!)* and Discovery and the Travel Channel, shop at Land's End and R.E.I., and have become the first generation in human history to believe that the wilderness is now safer than human civilization.

Whether we actually get very far in our seeking is beside the point—we like to think we do. *Life is a journey,* says Nissan, *enjoy the ride.* Mazda, knowing the pace at which we lead our lives, says simply, *Zoom, zoom, zoom.* Microsoft asks us, *Where do you want to go today?* And of course, if our journeys lead us astray and we find ourselves in a mess, Southwest Airlines asks us, *Wanna get away?*

The story of the magi is a story about seekers after God whose maps have failed them, who must dare to make their journey by starlight, and who blaze a trail that, as it turns out, first leads them about ten miles from their ultimate destination.

But it is also a story that is so tightly wrapped in myth and half-truths that it is hard to hear the simple truth within it. So much has been made of a story that, in truth, we know very little about. Poets such as T. S. Eliot and William Butler Yeats have written classical poems about these characters. The Christmas crèches on our mantles have them posing at the manger, next to angels and shepherds and sheep, bearing their gifts of gold, frankincense, and myrrh in the bucolic setting of the stable. Even our Christmas carols are misleading, calling them three kings from the Orient.

But we know very little about them, really. Matthew is the only gospel that, in all honesty, tells their story, and he neither calls them kings nor counts their numbers. We do not know who they were, or how many of them made the journey, or even where they came from. What is present-day Iraq was their likely homeland, but that certainly does not strengthen their case these days. We also do not know how long it took them to get to Bethlehem, or how old Jesus actually was when they arrived, though some biblical scholars suggest that it may have taken them a year, perhaps two, to get there. Matthew says that they found the holy family—not in a stable or a cave—but in a house, and he does not make mention of Joseph, whose paternity leave had perhaps already expired.

When you strip the biblical story clean from all the legends that have been attached to it over the years, perhaps you can see these "wise men" for who they are. They are human beings, like you and me, on a spiritual journey—a quest for something holy, something more powerful and meaningful than what their ordinary lives were offering them. They felt the undeniable tug and pull of God to search it out, despite the fact that they did not exactly know what they were looking for, or what they would do once they found it. And Matthew says they had a sign—a star hanging in the dark sky over a place they had never before journeyed—and a dream that stirred in them an enduring passion to press on until they arrived.

The dream was actually right out of the pages of the Old Testament. The magi were most likely aware of a poem, found in Isaiah 60, which was written nearly 500 years earlier for the Jews who were in exile. For more than two generations, those Jews longed for a return to Jerusalem. But Jerusalem, they learned, had been destroyed—the temple, the economy, the people, the city. It was a devastating moment in the history of God's chosen people. They despaired, they wept, they nearly lost hope. That was when a prophet wrote this little poem to them, as a way to encourage them— *"Arise, shine, for your light has come, / and the glory of the* LORD *has risen upon you… / Nations shall come to your light, / and kings to the brightness of your dawn"* (Isa. 60:1, 3). This poet renewed their hope, announcing that Jerusalem would be restored, that it would become a lighthouse to which people of all nations would be drawn. He gave them a vision for the future, and that future included good trade, prosperity, God's promise, and a central role on the world scene. It's going to happen, he said—it will take some time, but it will happen. A new king will appear, and he will return Jerusalem to its former splendor.[1] The magi apparently knew about that dream, and when they saw the star at its rising, they packed their camels and set out for the long journey. It was the light that Isaiah said would come. This was the moment. *Grab the gifts, the gold, the rare spices, it's time to pay homage to this new king.*

It took them a while to get there, but they were unfettered, full of hope, with stars in their eyes. They went right to the king's palace, thumped on the door, and when they took out their expensive gifts and showed them to the king's men, they were ushered straight to Herod. But this man, they knew right away, was the wrong guy. This is not what they had imagined. This king looked finished, not fresh; his own star seemed to have already fallen, and there was nothing about him that looked or sounded anointed. He looked very scary. In fact, he looked very scared.

"A new king," asked Herod? "You're looking for a new king? Hold on a minute," he said, and he left the room quickly and sat down with his scholars. "What are these wise guys talking about—a new king?" That is when Herod's Bible experts told him that the magi had it all wrong; they had only read half the story. You have to go to the book of Micah to get the full story, they said. So they told Herod about a passage from Micah, another prophet, who said that when the new king is born, he'll show up in *Bethlehem*, which was about ten miles away. One of them cleared his throat, dusted off the page of the scroll, and read to him Micah 5:2:

> But you, O Bethlehem of Ephrathah...
> from you shall come forth for me
>   one who is to rule in Israel,
> whose origin is from of old.

The scholars told him not to worry, that it was such an obscure little passage that it was no cause for concern. But it still scared the heck out of Herod, because if it *was* true, it meant that Herod's days were numbered. If indeed this new king was coming, it meant the old king was going. Herod raced back to the magi and told them, "Find that king. Immediately. And when you find him, come straight back here and tell me where he is. I'd *really* like to meet him..."

The magi did not wait around for Herod to finish. They knew something was not right about the place, and they never wanted to return, even if they did find what they were looking for down in Bethlehem. They packed their camels once again, and made the ten-mile journey to Bethlehem, to the place over which their star stood still. Only this place was no king's palace, but a simple shanty; and the king they found was no man at all, but a small child, nursing at his mother's breast. Despite the unconvincing physical evidence, Matthew says they knew they had found their king. Instead of offering butt wipes and baby rattles, they knelt down at Mary's rocking chair, laid out their royal gifts, and worshiped.

That is the real story behind the story. The magi first missed their mark before they finally found it, and this is what makes the story so frightening, and so revealing. The magi followed the star, but that star did not at first lead them to the right place. Instead of finding God, they found a Herod who would be their God if they let him.

Take great care with the stars you follow in this world. Not all of them lead to God, even when you think you know the story, the facts; even when a star leads you to a great palace that seems like a place where God would choose to dwell. Things are not always what they seem. Sometimes we miss the mark and end up ten miles from the real thing.

And we are a culture with stars in our eyes. The bright lights of the world attract us like moths to a porch light; only sometimes the luring light turns out to be a bug zapper that ends our journey long before it ever really begins. Augustine said we tend to worship that which we adore in this world, yet so much of what we worship often steals the light from our eyes and leaves us blind.

Wealth can do that. People seem to be attracted to wealth in this culture, and seem to do just about anything to get it. Some even believe it is a blessing, only to discover that once they have found it, it feels more like a burden. It is a star we tend to follow in this world, and it often keeps us ten miles from Bethlehem.

People can do that, too. Smart people, powerful people, famous people, the rising stars of pop culture—politicians, celebrities, Joe Millionaires, and American Idols—they all seem to catch our attention in this world. Maybe it is because we want to be like them; maybe it is because we want a piece of what they have. Whatever it is, I believe we pay them far more homage than we should in this culture.

Religion can do that, too. I know that sounds odd for a preacher to say, but religion can be a star that doesn't always lead us to God.

Sometimes we do religious things in order to avoid doing the things of God. Fred Craddock once recalled those students who never made it through seminary, apparently losing touch with their faith: They spent so much time talking about God, he said, that they forgot to talk to God. Religion can be a star that does not necessarily lead us to God. Both John the Baptist and Jesus were killed because they said as much.

We are a deeply spiritual generation that sometimes confuses good things with God things. We call *spiritual* experiences God, when often these experiences only point to the God we never meet. The rock band, Live, declares in their song "Heaven": "I don't need no one to tell me about heaven; I look at my daughter, and I believe."[2]

Maybe that theology works in the maternity ward; newborn babies have a way of making believers out of us. But having three children of my own, I can say that the heavenly feeling doesn't last. A few days into it, it feels like a lot of work—fifteen diapers a day, two feedings at night, night after night. I do not call that heaven. The trips to the ER, the endless time-outs, the carpools, the tears, the tonsillectomy, the homework, the broken hearts, the waiting up all night when she does not come home at curfew—this is not heaven, I am sorry to say.

My point, of course, is that for most of us, getting to Bethlehem is a matter of knowing the difference not only between Herod and the Holy One, but knowing, too, the difference between the things we call holy in this world and the One who is holier still. The stars we follow can lead us to Herod's palace as easily as they can lead us to Bethlehem. It is easy to take the wrong road. We open our treasure chests and give away our gold to lesser gods.

The magi could have stayed in Jerusalem. They could have simply opened their treasure chests and poured out their gold right there, without saying a word. Maybe that is part of the miracle of the story, that they did not stay; that after a very long, slow journey, after missing their mark, the stars in their eyes still led them on for another ten miles to seek the one thing they could not live without. But maybe, too, there is another miracle in the story—that which speaks of the awesome consequence of having finally met the One whom they were seeking. Maybe the real miracle of the story is that after having found him and worshiped him, they left for home by another road—the road that did not lead back to Herod's palace.

After Mary had put the baby back to bed and Joseph re-fueled the camels, I imagine that the magi walked outside to discover that their star in the sky would no longer be the star to lead them. That star had served its purpose, and now they would have to be led by another star, less visible on the outside, but radiating instead from within their own hearts. The gifts they had given their king had been matched by a far greater gift—the gift of direction.

Video Clip Suggestion

Phenomenon (Touchstone Pictures, 1996)

As George talks to the two children of the woman he loves, both of whom have recently learned that George has come to their home to die, he uses an apple as a prop and teaches the children that *"Everything is on its way to somewhere,"* and that life and love, when we allow them in, become part of us, even when they're gone (1:45:32—1:47:08).

Every Here and Now

Isaiah 40:21–31

Have you not known? Have you not heard? / Has it not been told you from the beginning? / Have you not understood from the foundations of the earth? / It is he who sits above the circle of the earth. (Isa. 40:21–22a)

So I go to the dermatologist last year to have some suspicious-looking spots on my back checked out. It's my annual inspection; about as routine as a lube job and tire rotation. Some of you lily-white folk know what I'm talking about. So the doctor looks me over real good—checks my back, my finely chiseled chest, my arms and legs, the tops of my feet. It's kind of like going through security at the airport now, right? They should get a search warrant before checking some of these places on your body. She goes through my hair like a chimp preening her young, looking for bugs, you know? Then her eyes lock on to my forehead, and the area around my eyes. She gives the area a long, heavy stare, and then lets out a sad, thoughtful sigh. I hold my breath. She's found something, I am sure. I immediately convince myself it's skin cancer; she's going to have to remove my face to get it all. I'm thinking I'm a goner when she says, with utter seriousness, "We can do something about all this, you know?" I am confused. *All of this? All of what?* "Something?" I ask. "What?" "Botox," she says. "All these deep furrows. All these early signs of crow's feet. The frown lines. Botox can achieve remarkable results on a face like yours." That's nice, isn't it? A face like mine is what Botox was made for.

Botox? The name itself sounds too much like buttocks, if you ask me, and I'd prefer to have neither anywhere near my face. *Botox.*

I had never heard of this stuff before last year. I asked her, "What's the deal with Botox?" So she tells me that Botox is a bacterium that is injected into your face; it's a form of botulism. Doctors shoot it into your face, and apparently this is a good thing—so good people will even pay good money for it. *Botox*. Once injected, this stuff attaches to the nerve endings in your face so that they will not allow those areas of your face to flex or "scrunch up" anymore. It will remove unwanted wrinkles, banish unsightly neckbands, and clear away irksome crow's feet, giving you a more youthful appearance. Botox basically paralyzes the nerves so they don't work anymore. That's nice, isn't it? You go to a party and someone cracks a joke but you can't for the life of you give up even a grin. You're laughing, but your face is as stiff as a statue. Some of you know exactly what I'm talking about.

If only we could erase the evidence of the past, or cover up the emotional aches of our present life; dull the senses, paralyze the nerves, feel nothing but numbness. According to my dermatologist, I'd look a lot better if I did that—at least for three months. That's about as long as Botox lasts. Then the wrinkles and frown lines come back, and your true identity is revealed. *The lines on our face, they say, are a map to our soul.*

U2 has a song on their *Pop* album entitled "Numb," in which Edge warns us not to grab or clutch or hope for too much, to avoid asking the hard questions and trying to make sense of our disillusionments. In the deadness of life, he cries out for more of that numbing stuff—"*Gimme some more of that stuff.*"[1]

There is an addiction to numbness in our culture, a fear of feeling too much. *Gimme some more of that stuff* to numb myself from feeling the aches and pains of life, to keep me from getting hurt, to protect me from myself, my struggles, my not-so-perfect life. Some numb themselves with a bottle of Bushmills or a needle and spoon. Some numb themselves with busyness, with frantic doing, rushing for a rush to cover the loneliness of rest. Some numb themselves by spending, consuming; some by the consumption of people, otherwise known as sex. Some go numb by overworking; some by over-playing. Some even numb themselves, I dare say, by religion—with its easy answers and cheap grace and manipulative promises that Jesus would have nothing to do with.

There is a numbness—a spiritual deadness—among the Israelites in our reading today. Their hearts have been injected with a toxic despair administered by the Babylonians, who hold them captive. Isaiah 40 offers a glimpse of that experience. The people are in exile. They have been carted off by the Babylonians as slaves; uprooted from their homes, their land, their identity as the people of Yahweh. The temple at Jerusalem has been destroyed. Everything they have ever known about God; everything they have ever believed about God; every hope, every promise, every pillar of faith has been leveled. The whole house of faith has come tumbling down around them. In Babylon, faith in Yahweh does not seem possible. They have been in captivity for more than a generation. Those who were carted off as children are now adults, aging and tired and full of dying memories of what used to be; their parents and grandparents have died; their children have inherited a faith that does not seem to work anymore.

If you ask me, these exiles that Isaiah speaks to in the reading this morning are not unlike you and me. They lived in an age of tremendous cultural transition. The world they once knew had changed. Their world had expanded. They went from the promised land, where God permeated every experience of life in tangible, visible ways—through ritual, through the temple, through the practice of torah—to a foreign, pluralistic land of many "gods," and Yahweh didn't seem to be one of them. They were spiritually homeless. Far from home, they could not make their old religion work anymore. The answers did not work; God did not seem to be present there; doubts crept in; their faith had serious holes in it; and they felt like they were sinking. Where was God? How could God allow this to happen to us? Was Yahweh really the Lord of Lords, or just another one of these local "gods" who could not work beyond the boundaries of home?

Psalm 137 is a psalm written in exile. You can hear the despair and resignation in Psalm 137. "By the rivers of Babylon— / there we sat down and there we wept / when we remembered Zion. / On the willows there / we hung up our harps... / How could we sing the Lord's song / in a foreign land?" (Ps. 137:1–2, 4).

We live in a culture of disbelief. We may be "one nation under God," but North America is actually a smoldering pit of skepticism when it comes to belief in God. In the book *Celebrities in Hell*, Warren Allen Smith offers an irreverent compendium of famous freethinkers, which includes, as he says, "agnostics, atheists, naturalists, pragmatists, secular humanists, or nontheists of some stripe." "We were not created by a deity," chimes Phyllis Diller. "We created the deity in our image. Life began on this planet when the first amoeba split." Carrie Fisher adds, "I love the idea of God, but it's not stylistically in keeping with the way I function." Nick Nolte declares, "I have difficulty with God and with beliefs. You have to ask yourself the question, 'If God created man in his own image, what kind of an image is God?'" But perhaps the most honest statement comes from Matt Groening, who says, "Technically, I'm an agnostic, but I definitely believe in hell—especially after watching the fall TV schedule."[2]

The movie *Signs* captures some of this skepticism and open dismissal of faith. Mel Gibson stars as Graham Hess, a minister who has lost his faith after the tragic death of his wife in a car accident. When strange signs are carved into his cornfields and unidentified aircraft appear in the sky, the entire county begins to panic. Hess and his brother Merrill have a discussion about what they think is going on, and whether it's a matter of fate or providence.

Isaiah has the courage to let the questions sit there—to acknowledge the questions, to let them be asked, to not run from them. Is this all just an accident? Is life itself just a long series of coincidences? Is someone really in charge, or are we left to go it alone in this world? The Israelites never asked those questions until they were stripped from their homes, from their land—the land that God gave them—and had to face life in a foreign, hostile land where no one cared about Yahweh. Where is God? Is there someone looking out for us?

There are at least two ways we can answer such questions. The first way is to say that what we do and who we become in life are simply a matter of luck. Sometimes we catch a break; sometimes we don't. There is good luck, they say, and there is bad luck, and much of the time it is out of our control. The Greeks believed in the Fates, those women who sat at their spinning wheels in heaven, each spinning a person's life thread, and when one of their threads broke, the poor soul down on Earth would die.

Maybe you know some people who subscribe to this theory. They are the kind of people who say, "I can't do that because the right opportunity has never presented itself," or they say, "This happened out of pure luck." They are content on allowing chance and circumstance to determine the outcome of their lives.

But there is another way of answering the questions. Isaiah chooses this way. He says, first of all you have to ask the questions, because the questions are the surest sign that the Botox is wearing off and you're finally feeling something, even if that something is pain, or sadness, or heartbreak. Ask the questions. Speak your doubts. Do not be afraid of them. Just do not expect to get the answers in the form of any hard evidence, any proof beyond your own understanding of scripture, tradition, and your own experience. "His understanding is unsearchable…"

This is what I love about Isaiah. This is why I think Isaiah could have been a preacher today. He is unafraid to point to the undeniable, unmistakable mystery of God. He is not trying to give you four keys or twenty-one principles or twelve laws for believing in God. He is not into answers; he is into experience. He is not into religion; he is into a relationship with God that has to be seen, felt, heard, tasted. What does he say? "Look to the heavens. The one who made all that, the one who stretches open the heavens like a curtain and spreads them like a tent to live in—is here, even here, right here in this place, this seemingly God-forsaken land. We look like grasshoppers to God who breathes and the mightiest of kings falls over; we're all like seeds of grass—sown, and withering, all at once. God makes it all happen. Do not for an instant think that God cannot see you. You may be far from home, but God is present in every here and now, every now and then."

Isaiah believed in providence. He says the same God who hung the stars in the sky for a purpose is the God who knitted you in your mother's womb and numbered the hairs on your head and knows you through and through, because there is a purpose for you, and whether you realize it or not, whether you're at home or in exile in this world, God is working out God's purposes. It is not something to be figured out; no reasonable explanations will do. You must have eyes to see and ears to hear when it presents itself to you.

Where have you *seen* God at work in your life? in the world? What have you *heard, felt, experienced* that draws you to the mysteries of God, which cannot be explained, only trusted?

Isaiah says, "Have you not known? Have you not heard? / Has it not been told you from the beginning? / Have you not understood from the foundations of the earth? It is he who sits above the circle of the earth" (Isa. 40:21–22a).

A man hears a sermon one day, and something clicks. Decides he is willing to move "anywhere in the country" so as to have more time with his family. A position that will reset him in his pay tier— five levels below where he was. But after he gives his career to God and his family he ends up getting a raise. Company pays to relocate him in, of all places, his parents' hometown. He has a house six minutes walking distance from his work.[3]

"Have you not known? Have you not heard? Has it not been told you from the beginning? Have you not understood from the foundations of the earth? It is he who sits above the circle of the earth."

A family in the church came to me with a crisis. They have been very open about this story, by the way, which is why I dare share it with you. They came to me to consider their options. He is an attorney, she a homemaker; they have three small children. His private practice of ten years was going nowhere. One month of income seemed always to be followed by three months of living in the red. Bills went unpaid; debts continued to grow; savings accounts were depleted; the future looked bleak. The time had come to pull the plug on the practice, but the job market for attorneys was thin. Resumes went out but the phone calls never came. After twelve months of this, the tension in their marriage had brought them to a crossroads.

We talked about the options that night, and then we prayed. Before they left, they agreed to pray together, to daily place this burden in the hands of God, to trust, to love, to encourage one another. They left my office at nine o'clock that night. At ten o'clock the next morning, he called me. He had just hung up the phone after speaking with a firm that had held his resume for more than nine months. The interview was scheduled, the offer was accepted, and we knew right then that it is God who sits above the circle of the Earth.

I do not know that it always works that way, I only know what I have seen and heard, what has been told to me from the beginning, from the foundations of the earth. And I believe it. Call it luck. Call it fate. Call it circumstance. Call it what you will. I choose to call it the hand of God, and it is enough to make me pick up my harp under the willow tree and sing the Lord's song in this foreign land.

Video Clip Suggestion

Signs (Touchstone Pictures, 2002)

As news of the invasion flashes on the television screen, Graham Hess talks to his brother, Merrill, about faith, providence, and the presence of God. *"What kind of person are you—are you the kind of person who sees signs and miracles, or do you believe people just get lucky? Is it possible that there are no coincidences?"* (0:41:00—0:43:00).

As Graham and his family sit down for dinner, Graham's son suggests that "maybe we should have a prayer." Graham, who now questions his faith after the tragic death of his wife, refuses to pray, saying "I'm not wasting one more minute of my life on prayer—not one more minute" (1:10:00—1:13:00).

You Have No Idea

Mark 9:2–9

"This is my Son, the Beloved; listen to him!" (Mk. 9:7)

Anyone who has followed Jesus for any length of time has had to deal with that chronic, often maddening suspicion that it's not at all what you had expected. The sticky fish on the back of the car comes unglued. The bumper sticker theology begins to flake and peel. The dashboard Jesus melts in the glaring sun and the "Cross in My Pocket" charm gets lost in the wash. One day you wake up to discover the "Footprints in the Sand" look more like butt prints in wet concrete. Do you know what I'm talking about? Things don't go as planned, and you wonder—*Am I a fool, or does Jesus actually know what he's doing?* Admittedly, we do not have all the facts. When we follow Jesus, we operate on limited information. Even so, he does seem a lot like the Professor on Gilligan's Island, right? He can build a two-way radio out of coconuts and fashion a generator out of palm trees, but he never seems to get around to patching up that hole in the Skipper's boat so you can get back home.

A man is walking along the side of the cliff when he gets too close to the edge and falls off. On his way down he grabs a branch, which temporarily stops his fall. He can't hold on forever, so he starts yelling for help. And immediately a voice comes from above: "Hey, buddy, I'm right here. It's me, the Lord." "The Lord?" he asks. "You mean, God?" "Yep, I'm here to help you," says the Lord. "Anything, God, I'll do anything you say, just get me out of this." So the Lord says, "Okay, buddy, I know this is going to sound crazy, but I want you to let go of that branch. Don't worry, I'll catch you." The man says, "Let me get this straight—I've got two-hundred feet of airspace beneath me, and you want me to let go of this branch?" "Yep," says the Lord. "Just trust me. I'll catch you." The man thinks for a moment. There is a long, hard silence. Finally, the man yells, "Help! Is there anyone else up there?"

Have you been there? We all have, right? We know what God says, but there comes a time for all of us when it's hard to trust it, when you wonder if God is listening, if God gets it, if God is ever going to cooperate.

I am convinced that when each of us made the conscious decision to follow Jesus, we had no idea what we were getting into. Peter is representative of that. We can relate to Peter. He is a lot like us—quick to speak, slow to understand. He is so eager when he leaves his nets on the shores of Galilee to follow Jesus. He's a born leader who wants more out of life than a boat full of dead fish. Peter wants to change the world, and he believes he's found a man from Nazareth who is about to do it. Peter is part of a winning team. He can see it, taste it, feel it deep in his bones.

One day the disciples and Jesus have what we might call a "come to Jesus meeting" down in Caesarea Philippi. Up to this point, everything has been pretty cozy for the disciples. The healings, the miracles, the publicity—they all seem to be leading them somewhere that no one has gone before. Jesus is everything he's cracked up to be—a huge success, a rising star. But on this particular day, the wheels fall off. Jesus sits them down and asks them the one question that will change everything. "Who do people say that I am?" One of them says, "Elijah," another one says, "a prophet," someone from the back of the room says, "John Ashcroft." The class has a good laugh. And then Jesus says, "But who do you say that I am?" That's when Peter, without hesitation, says, "You are the Messiah."

That was no cheap title back then. It meant something. Messiah wasn't someone who could merely make a difference in the world. Messiah was someone who would make a different world altogether. Messiah was the one for whom the Jews had waited all their lives. Messiah was the king, who would restore justice and peace, who would overthrow the Romans, who would return the promised land to the people of God.

Peter believed he knew who Jesus was. He had him pegged for the warrior king who would set things straight, forever. Peter had plans for Jesus, which is why it must have felt like he had been hit by a train when Jesus told him he was wrong. Not about the Messiah business; Peter was right about that. But about what kind of Messiah Jesus was going to be. Instead of a victorious, mighty king, Jesus said the Son of Man must suffer, and be rejected, and be killed, and rise after three days. Peter only heard the first three—suffer, rejection, death. And on that terrible day down in Caesarea Philippi, he wondered how any suffering, rejected, dead man could call himself the Messiah.

Things are not always what they seem. You think you have finally got things figured out and life pulls the rug out from underneath you. Faith is supposed to lead you to green pastures, and you find yourself instead in the valley of the shadows. You pray for something to go well, something to go away, and it feels like your prayer comes back "return to sender." You expect Jesus to solve your problems, not create more of them. You leave behind your treasures on this earth and pledge to store up new treasures in heaven, only to find that when you open the safe to look inside, it's filled with ashes. Three years with Jesus, Peter thought to himself, and he drops the bomb on me—suffering, rejection, death.

So our scripture reading begins with these three words—"Six days later…" It is six days after that devastating day down in Caesarea Philippi when everything fell apart. Maybe Jesus sensed that Peter was ready to bail out. Maybe Jesus overheard Peter on his cell phone, calling his pop back in Galilee to see if he had room on his boat for a son who was ready to come home after three years on the road. Maybe Jesus just loved him so much that he felt it was time to show him. All we know is that Jesus took him, and James and John, up the mountain, just the four of them, to get away and figure things out. And something happened up there. Mark doesn't elaborate. All he says is that Jesus changed—his appearance, his clothes, everything. He was lit up like a nuclear powered night light, and the only word to describe it was "glory."

Then Moses and Elijah showed up and stood next to Jesus, and Peter felt like the kid in *Sixth Sense* who saw dead people. These were the big dogs, right? Moses was the great law giver, Elijah the king of prophets. Standing together, the three of them looked larger than life. Astonished, Peter tried to speak, but the consonants got stuck in his throat before he could form them into words. That's when he heard God's voice thunder down from heaven, like a James Earl Jones baritone, saying, "This is my son, the beloved, listen to what he says. He knows what he's doing."

What Peter was trying to say before God interrupted was that, if Jesus didn't mind, he'd like to keep him just like he is, all lit up in glory, and stay up on the mountain forever. To nail down that moment for all time—that would prove he wasn't wrong after all. To stay up on the hill and shine like a lighthouse—that might not *change* the world, Peter figured, but it would brighten it, and that seemed to be an acceptable alternative to the suffering, rejection, and death plan that Jesus had in mind.

And can you blame him? Peter loved Jesus more than he loved anything or anyone in this world, and the thought of losing him broke his heart in two. But there was also the public perception problem—who wants to follow a suffering, rejected, dead Messiah? Where's the hope in that? None of us, if put in the same position as Peter, would opt for Plan A. None of us wants to associate with losers, with the rejected, with has-beens and also-rans, which makes it all the more ironic that Christianity as a religion has endured for two thousand years. Jesus, after all, is not exactly a model for success in this world. He was born a peasant and died a criminal; was executed by the state in order to maintain the peace; his best friends abandoned him in his darkest hour; he preached abundant life, yet died penniless, at the age of about thirty-five; and the few followers he left behind suffered a similar fate. How has a movement with that kind of story line survived for this long?

There is a new phenomenon in many churches these days, especially the rapidly growing ones. Some of these churches, when they build their buildings, are intentionally leaving out the cross. You walk into these buildings—which are not called sanctuaries, by the way, but worship centers—and there are no visible reminders of suffering, rejection, death. Why? Because people don't come to church to get the willies, right? They come to feel good about themselves, to be reminded that they have a buddy named Jesus who will show them how to lead a successful, prosperous life. Stick with the glory; spare me the gore, because success sells today. It's a message of humanity without sin, of grace without the cross, and a kingdom without judgment.

But I will tell you the secret about this story we call the transfiguration. The glimpse of glory did not work. Peter didn't get it. The whole purpose of taking Peter and James and John up the mountain was to give them a glimpse of the very end of the story. It was God's way of letting these three take a peek at the last page of the book. Sure, there is a terrible, bloody fate waiting for Jesus when he comes back down this mountain, but that is not how the story is going to end, says God. Let me give you a peek. Look, there is Jesus, on the mountain, in full glory, just as he will be *after* the suffering, rejection, and death. *After* all of that, Jesus will appear in glory. Get it? But Peter and James and John trip down the windy mountain, confused and clueless about everything that had happened. They had no idea.

The truth of it is that the glory story doesn't work. Without the cross, no one can see the glory. If you read the entire gospel of Mark, no one really gets it that Jesus is the Messiah, the true Son of God. A few, like Peter, think they know. They are convinced by miracles and healings and speeches and photo shoots of Jesus with children and their pet hamsters. That looks like a pretty great guy, doesn't it? Jesus, our buddy, the Messiah. But no one, by looking at all the glorious stuff he does, understands. There is only one who does understand, and the revelation came to him at the cross. You will find him at the end of Mark's gospel, and you will note that he is not even a religious person. In fact, he is one of the executioners, a Roman centurion. Standing at the foot of the cross, gazing at this lifeless body hanging from a tree, he is the first to understand what no one for three years could see: "Truly this man was God's Son!" (Mk. 15:39).

What Mark is saying is that you cannot know Jesus apart from the suffering, rejection, and death. What he is saying is that we will know he is the real deal by his stripes, that you will know he is the Messiah not because he rescues you from the cliffs in life, but because he jumps over the side with you and promises not to leave you there alone.

Three days before my father died, we were still holding out hope that he'd come around, leave the hospital, buy more time. But the persistent cough proved that the cancer had moved to his lungs; it had started in the stomach and had already traveled to the liver.

The lungs were the final frontier, and he was in a bad way at that point. The young intern came in to tell him about the lung part, and to tell him that he wouldn't be going home, *ever*. I remember when he walked into the room; I held my breath, hoping his news would be good, that he would solve my father's problems. I also remember what he did after he told my father the bad news. He cried. He told me later that it was the first time he had ever had to tell a man that he was dying; he cried because there was nothing left to do but cry. He looked like Jesus, who also seemed unable to solve my father's problems, but shared them instead.

I cannot imagine a church without a cross, a Jesus without wounds, a God without suffering, glory without rejection, Easter without Good Friday. The way Mark tells the story, everyone tried— Peter, James, John, Judas, Pilate, the Pharisees, the crowds. But no one saw him, until the very end, when his suffering gave him away.

In a small hospital chapel in Isenheim, Germany, there was once a painting at the altar where patients, doctors, nurses and staff of that hospital came to pray. The painting was the work of the sixteenth-century artist, Mathias Grunewald. It was called a triptych, which meant that it was spread across three panels; the panel on the left and the panel on the right were on hinges, so they could be swung shut, covering the center panel. But these side panels were painted on both front and back, so that, when they were folded shut, they made up one scene, and when they were opened, an entirely different scene was revealed.

The Isenheim altarpiece reveals one of the most truthful interpretations of the story of Jesus. When the triptych is closed the two side panels show the crucified body of Jesus. He hangs there on the cross, his body broken and bleeding, the days of his young, hopeful life reduced to a moment of suffering. But when you swing open the two outer panels, there is revealed the brilliant figure of the risen Christ rendered by the artist in blazing tones of gold and white. The risen Christ has been released from the pain and suffering of the cross and rises triumphantly into the eternal.

But it is not the inside panel that convicts me; it is the crucifixion scene on those two outer panels, when the triptych is closed, that I cannot seem to get out of my mind.[1] When you take a closer look at the crucified form of Jesus, you notice that his body is scarred by something more than the traditional wounds of crucifixion. In addition to the nail holes and the other wounds, Jesus appears to be suffering from a strange disease, his body is covered randomly with what appear to be skin lesions.

In their research into Grunewald's work, art historians have discovered that during the sixteenth century when the artist painted the altarpiece, thousands of people in Germany were dying of a strange, as yet undiagnosed disease. And the prominent features of this progressive and incurable new disease were the lesions by which the artist has conveyed Christ's own suffering. The artist seems to be saying that Jesus has taken upon himself the suffering of the people. Though it went undiagnosed at the time, this peculiar disease was later given a name—syphilis, the venereal disease that German explorers had carried back with them from the new world.

> But he was wounded for our transgressions,
>   crushed for our iniquities;
> upon him was the punishment that made us whole,
>   and by his bruises we are healed…
> He was oppressed, and he was afflicted,
>   yet he did not open his mouth;
> like a lamb that is led to the slaughter,
>   and like a sheep that before its shearers is silent,
>   so he did not open his mouth.
> By a perversion of justice he was taken away.
>   Who could have imagined his future?
>   (Isa. 53:5, 7–8a)

Who could have imagined? We had no idea.

Video Clip Suggestion

Ice Age (20th Century Fox, 2002)

Manny risks his life while rescuing Diego from a collapsing ice bridge. When Diego, who is secretly planning to kill Manny and Sid, asks Manny why he risked his life to save him, Manny replies, "That's what you do in the herd—you look out for each other." Sid comments, "I don't know about you guys, but we are the weirdest herd I have ever seen" (0:52:00—0:56:00).

PART 2

Suffering

"The creative action of the Christian's life," wrote Flannery O'Connor, "is to prepare his death in Christ. It is a continuous action in which the world's goods are utilized to the fullest."[1] Diagnosed with lupus shortly after completing her first novel, O'Connor came to embrace her illness as an extraordinary gift that contributed to her vocation as an artist. Before her death at the age of thirty-nine, she wrote of the "passive diminishments"—a phrase borrowed from Teilhard de Chardin—suggesting that our spiritual character is formed as much by what we endure and what is taken from us as it is by our achievements and conscious choices. This became a dominant theological theme played out in many of her fictional characters, who were stripped both of their sins as well as their apparent virtues in order to arrive at a deeper truth and a more honest self-awareness.

I confess that I do not know how to preach O'Connor's "passive diminishments" while attempting to grow a church these days. Even O'Connor acknowledged that "people don't realize how much religion costs. They think faith is a big electric blanket, when of course it is the cross."[2] Not much has changed. Many churches in North America, especially the newer, larger ones, have elected to keep the cross in the closet in favor of a more palatable, capable faith. It is one thing to talk about the redemptive suffering of Jesus, but it is quite another to invite our listeners to participate in it as a means of "preparing our death in Christ."

We live in a therapeutic age in which our suffering can be fixed, our scars erased, our life spans extended, our deaths postponed. Yet our Christian vocation calls us to embrace our suffering as a legacy—to become the body and blood of Christ, as our communion liturgy affirms: blessed, broken, poured out for the world. I believe that Christians of the emerging generation find in the suffering of Jesus a depth of solidarity that gives meaning and purpose to their own present sufferings, and I suggest that it is the task of the church to proclaim a word of grace that neither denies nor fixes their suffering, but redeems it and offers it to the world as bread.

The sermons in this unit invite the listener to reflect on what it means to embrace the cross as the principle, yet foolish, symbol of redemption; to choose suffering as our Christian legacy; to endure unwanted suffering as a blessing; and to perceive our scars as the viable and compelling evidence of resurrection in Christ.

All That You Can't Leave Behind

Mark 8:31–38

"If any want to become my followers, let them deny themselves and take up their cross and follow me." (Mk. 8:34b)

On the dry Laetoli plain of northern Tanzania in 1977, archaeologist Mary Leakey found a trail of footprints belonging to some of the earliest known humans to have ever lived. The three barefoot people—likely a short man and woman and child—walked closely together. They walked on moist volcanic tuff and ash on a day about 3.6 million years ago, and today we have a record of that moment in time. After they walked across this plain, more ash covered their footprints and later hardened. We know that as they walked together, it was raining, because next to their footprints are the pockmarks of the rain also preserved by the fallen ash. We have about ninety feet of that family's steady footprints intact. We do not know where they were going or why, but it's likely that, as the great Sadiman volcano erupted and destroyed much of their land, they were fleeing their home in search of safer ground. Wherever they were walking, we know that as they walked, the woman paused and turned left, walking briefly in a different direction, only to turn back and rejoin her family.[1] Perhaps she had a moment of doubt; perhaps she was taking a last look back at the place they were leaving behind; perhaps she was looking for another trail into her future. We do not know. We know only that whatever it was that caused her to turn away was not enough to keep her away, and that wherever they went, then went there together.

It's curious, isn't it, that the oldest footprints ever discovered are footprints belonging to three people who were running away from something? We don't know where they went; but we do know that they were running away from home, running in search of safety, in the face of something they could not manage, could not control.

Apparently, running away from danger, searching for safer ground, is a natural human instinct. It is called self-preservation, and who among us, in the face of danger and uncertainty and fear, doesn't consider a similar strategy? When the volcanoes erupt in our lives—when the painful, unexpected storms blow through our lives and set us on our ears—we look for the safest, most pain-free alternatives, don't we?

I'm talking about the trials all of us encounter in our lives, and the way we either face them head-on or run from them with tails high. Life is full of them; we've all had them; and we all know that our first instinct is to run from them for fear of being defeated by them, or painfully changed by them.

It happened one day for one well-respected family. The father served on one of the church boards; the mother taught Sunday school; their teenage daughter was one of the most popular kids in the youth group. One day the house went up on the market; a job transfer to another state was quickly arranged; and the moving company blew into town overnight and was gone the next day. And they, along with their sixteen-year-old daughter, who was now three-months pregnant, were headed to Iowa before anyone knew they were gone.

Do you know what I am talking about? It is the age-old human instinct of fight or flight, and most of the time we choose the latter, for fear of not having what it takes to face our trials head-on, opting instead for the safest, most comfortable way out.

We set out in life hoping to find a pain-free, trouble-free, satisfaction-guaranteed life. And one day you're doing the laundry and stumble upon a bag of weed in your ninth-grader's jeans pocket; or one day your marriage is shattered and strewn across the rocks of infidelity or indifference or adversity; or one day the X-ray comes back with some terrifying, dark, malignant mass; or one day the pink slip shows up on the desk you've worked at for twelve long, faithful years, and security walks you to the door. And you wonder if—*how*—you will ever get through this in one piece, with your dignity and faith and life in one piece. And you ask—why? Why me? Why now? Why this? And then you search frantically through the house that is your life, looking for a back door, a way out, a way into something that looks like anything other than the mess that has suddenly piled chin-high around you.

You come to church, because church is supposed to help in times like this; you come looking for that way out, looking for a lifeline that will save you from all of this mess—something, someone, who will resolve your problems and take them away—and instead you get this seemingly impossible, unsympathetic word from Jesus that says that you actually have to *bear* this cross; that you cannot run away from this, that you cannot leave this behind, that the only way out of it is straight through it. And you wonder, where's the hope in that? Jesus says, "We all have crosses to bear; some are harder, heavier, more burdensome than others. But with every cross comes the promise of a resurrection. With every cross we bear, with every little death we endure, there is an empty tomb on the other side." If only we do not run away from it first.

From what I can tell, it is the hardest word Jesus ever spoke, and it is the one impossible word the church is so afraid to speak in this self-help, pop-psychology, saccharine-theology age of preaching. So bear with me. I do not necessarily like this word anymore than you do, because it hurts, and I know few, including myself, who would argue that cross-bearing is anything but painful, and the very last thing we would choose. *A cross?* What about a balm in Gilead, to make the wounded whole? What about following all the rules, doing good, believing all the right things, and getting rewarded for it? Isn't there some immunity to pain inherent in the Christian way of life? Isn't Jesus supposed to protect us from the things that hurt us? But all Jesus talks about is a cross.

Do not sentimentalize this cross business. When Jesus said you had to bear your cross, he wasn't talking about some 14-karat gold symbol you wear around your neck. The cross had no religious meaning yet; in fact, it was an image of violence and terror. The cross Jesus was talking about was the primary instrument of execution of his day, and his disciples had seen more than a few of them anchored to busy street corners, with criminals hanging from them, suffering a slow, terrifying death. It was the Romans' way of intimidating you—an emotional cattle prod that zapped some sense into you if you had any intentions of rising up against the state. So when he talked about a cross, he was talking about the most feared form of death of his day—the very thing people should do everything in their power to *avoid* at all costs.

"Take up your cross and follow," he said. Which was another way of saying, "Whatever you fear most in life, don't let it pull your chain—cancer; a job loss; a seemingly impossible task or circumstance; an unavoidable decision; a frustrating relationship; an unwanted, undesirable event." Jesus says, *You can bear this. I know you don't want to; I know you wouldn't choose this; but if it's yours, you can bear this. It's not as scary as you think. I know it seems scary. I know it seems impossible. But it's not impossible. Don't run away from it; instead, take it with you.*

A Beautiful Mind is based on the story of John Forbes Nash Jr.—a mathematical genius crippled by the harrowing disease of schizophrenia. His disease devastates his life and his family. In one scene, his wife Alicia, fearing her safety, has made the difficult decision to leave him. But on her way out of the house, she turns around, and faces her fears with courage and hope.

"I want to believe that something extraordinary can happen," she says. And don't we all, in *our* most difficult hour, want the same. The truth that Jesus is trying to get through to us is that, for something extraordinary to happen, you cannot run from the crosses in your life. You have to bear them up on your shoulders and walk. There are some things you cannot leave behind; crosses are meant to be borne up, not buried.

I think Paul the apostle was trying to say the same thing to the Christians in Rome years later, as they faced a few crosses of their own: "For I am convinced that neither death, nor life, nor angels, nor rulers, nor things present, nor things to come, nor powers, nor height, nor depth, nor anything else in all creation, will be able to separate us from the love of God in Christ Jesus our Lord" (Rom. 8: 38–39).

What Paul didn't say was what Jesus *did* say in today's passage. Jesus was saying that, "There is nothing in this world that can separate you from me, except one thing that is entirely under your control. The only thing in this world that can separate you from me is, of course, *you*. You can run from your fears; or you can crawl underneath them, and bear them on your shoulders, and walk on. If you want to be my disciples, you will choose door number two. It will cost you something. But you can do it. You can. Because what is impossible for humans is possible with God."

If you want to believe that something extraordinary can happen in the midst of your painful struggles, then put yourself in the path of an extraordinary God who will meet you there. God does not promise to take the cross from you, but does promise to bear it with you, and promises that beyond every cross is life.

Will Willimon tells the poignant story of a family who took this cross-bearing business for real. Their baby had been born with Down's syndrome and the doctor expressed concern about the "suffering" such a child would bring the family.

> "Suffering?" [the mother] said quietly. "We appreciate your concern, but we're Christians. God suffered for us, and we will try to suffer for the baby, if we must"…
>
> Two days later, the doctor and I watched the couple leave the hospital. They walked slowly, carrying a small bundle; but it seemed a heavy burden to us, a weight on their shoulders. We felt as if we could hear them dragging, clanking it down the front steps of the hospital, moving slowly but deliberately into a cold, gray March morning…
>
> But as they left, I noticed a curious look on their faces; they looked as if the burden were not too heavy at all, as if it were a privilege and a sign. They seemed borne up, as if on another's shoulders, being carried toward some high place the doctor and I would not be going, following a way we did not understand.[2]

"Nothing can separate us from the love of God," said Paul. "What is impossible for humans is possible with God," said Jesus. You can do this.

Do you want to believe that something extraordinary is possible? Then take off your running shoes, turn around and face your fears, and climb back up that mountain, dragging that cross of yours behind you. There's life up there: abundant, fearless, extraordinary life. And there are people like you and me who will go there with you, carrying our own crosses, helping you carry yours, looking for the Life that has a name—Jesus.

Video Clip Suggestion

A Beautiful Mind (Universal Pictures, 2001)

As Alicia prepares to leave her schizophrenic husband, John Nash, she has a change of heart and confesses to John that she wants "to believe that something extraordinary can happen" (1:43:00—1:46:00).

The Time of Your Life

John 12:20–33

"Unless a grain of wheat falls into the earth and dies, it remains just a single grain." (Jn. 12:24)

Last week I buried the last of my four grandparents. My grandmother died two weeks ago today, right about the time I stood before you to preach. Moments before I preached that morning, as we were singing the middle hymn at our second service, I had a clear vision of my grandmother's face, which, at the time, I did not understand. A few hours later, when I walked through the front door, Lori said to me, "Your aunt just called. There's bad news." I already knew what Lori was about to say.

Five days later we gathered at the graveside and gave my grandmother back to God. All the family saints who have gone before me are buried there at that cemetery. My uncle is there; he died five months before I was born, in the jungles of Vietnam in March of 1968. Two grandfathers—and now two grandmothers—are there, one great aunt rests beside them, and a hundred yards up on the hill rests my father, who watches over them like a young sentinel at his post.

It was the first graveside service my children had ever witnessed. Alyson seemed to take it all in stride, as if she understood. Casey was more concerned and curious, like Columbo attempting to solve a new mystery. He walked right up to that dark hole in the earth, looked down, and gave me a knowing glance. He grabbed hold of my hand and squeezed hard. Then he let go, turned around, and skipped across a few dozen headstones, playing hopscotch on the faces of the saints. I could hear the sounds of angels laughing as he tiptoed over each of them.

When you see the fresh hole in the ground, and breathe in the moist, fertile smell of the soil, and feel the spring sun shine down upon the place, it feels more like the planting of a seed than the burying of a body. A funeral is as much a beginning as it is an ending. You bury a life in the earth and find what strength you can to wait out the long season of grief and loss. Then one day that seed sprouts. You look down and see a legacy breaking through the surface—first just a single leaf, then something that looks like a full stock of wheat stretching toward the sky, reaching out for sunlight and air, until at just the right time in your life it begins to bear the fruit, the grain that gives itself up freely, over time, to feed the lives of those who are left behind.

The world measures a life by the years it lives and the fruit that it produces in the here and now; Jesus measures a life by the legacy it leaves behind. Every life that has ever lived, every life that you and I are given to live with the time that we are given to live it, has within it the very stuff that one day will produce a legacy that will feed the lives of those who come after us, if we will dare to freely offer it. What will be the legacy of your life? What fruit will this seed that is your life ultimately bear, once it is finally planted in earth and history, time and space?

Jesus wanted us to know that those who seek to be like him in this world will see their lives as holy seeds that one day will be given back to the earth, planted, in order to bear fruit for those who come after us. "Unless a grain of wheat falls into the earth and dies," he says, "it remains just a single grain. But if it dies, it bears much fruit." The seed he happened to be talking about was no ordinary seed at all. He was talking about the seed of his very life. What he was saying was that while his life in this world was of great significance, it was rather small and fleeting when compared to the eternal legacy it would leave behind through his death. His whole life was given to him for a higher purpose—to make wheat, to bear a kind of fruit with his life that would endure even beyond the brief life he was given to live. His life was a seed; his unique fruit, salvation—the eternal legacy we inherit as sons and daughters of God.

The twelfth chapter of John signals a dramatic turn in Jesus' life. When he arrived in Jerusalem for the Passover festival, he knew he would be wearing a bull's-eye on his back. He was now a marked man; his days were now numbered. Jesus had a decision to make, although the way John tells the story, it wasn't a decision that caused him anguish. He had before him two choices—to preserve at all costs the good name the world had given him, or to make wheat in the world, despite the high probability that it would come at a very high cost. The first choice would buy him time; the latter, a legacy.

According to John, Jesus was already well on his way to making a name for himself. He had quickly become the lead story on the evening news from Galilee all the way to Jerusalem, and everywhere he traveled he left behind the evidence of his presence and impact—jars of Merlot from a wedding in Cana; the healed son of a royal official skating on roller blades in Capernaum; scattered loaves of bread on the eastern shores of Tiberias; the empty mat of a once-lame man at Bethzatha; the open eyes of a once-blind man at Siloam; and a once-dead man named Lazarus dancing in burial rags at Bethany. No doubt about it, Jesus had made a name for himself, and the evidence of his impact on the locals was both compelling and tangible. Skeptics believed, the crippled walked, the hungry were filled, and the dead and the good-as-dead rose from their tombs.

But the evidence he left behind became the very trail of evidence the religious establishment would use against him. His open defiance of tradition, his public confrontations with the religious authorities, his bold claims about his unique relationship to God all sounded like heresy to the leaders of his day. He began to look a lot like a dangerous rebel that must be stopped immediately, at all costs. *He cannot be allowed to go on this way*, they said. He had drawn people to God by calling them away from their hollow forms of religion. He had called the religious leaders liars and thieves. *If we let him continue with these words and miracles, everyone will believe him*, they concluded. So they decided to take him down, to arrest him and kill him and return to business as usual.

When he arrived in Jerusalem, the pack of wolves sent scouts to track him. That's when Jesus had a moment of truth in his life. He could save his good name by compromising his mission, or he could cling to his mission and likely lose his life. The first option would require him to head for the hills, or hide out in the city, or sell out by choosing his words a little more carefully. Had he chosen this option, there's little doubt he could have touched a few more lives while preserving his own life—and who could ever blame him for that? *You've got to know when to hold 'em, and know when to fold 'em,* right?

But, of course, he chose the latter option—the choice of self-giving, because he loved God more than he loved his life, and he knew that he could either save his life but lose his legacy, or give up his life in order to make one.

Jesus is the only one in all of history who would have to die in order to offer the world the legacy of salvation. No one else can ever make such a claim; no one else will ever have to. But Jesus believed that all of us who have inherited that legacy would have to make some hard choices if our lives are to count for something more than the simple meaning the world gives them. It is *one* hard choice, really, made again and again over the course of our lives—the choice between self-preservation and self-offering, the choice between hanging on to things the world deems important, or letting go of them in order to inherit something far greater. You can choose the first, said Jesus, and maybe leave behind an estate, a trust fund, a pot of gold that will one day run dry; or you can choose the second option, and leave behind a legacy that will feed the world.

I have known people who have chosen the first, and known people who have chosen the latter. I've sat with all of them in their last days of life, and I have buried them, too. You can generally tell which choice they have made by the peace with which they face their end. But the truth of their choice, the proof of it, is most often reflected by the peace in the lives of the people they have left behind, or the lack of it. Not every life leaves a legacy; some leave burdens that never seem to be lifted from the backs of those who mourn them. I have buried the dead with no one present but the groundskeeper and the idling backhoe; and I have buried the dead in the presence of those faithful who gather there to inherit their legacy. And I have learned over the years that a legacy will cost you something, just as it cost Jesus something. It may not be your life, as it was for Jesus, but it will be a costly part of your life—something that once given up cannot be taken back. Something so costly that the legacy it purchases in the process is priceless and irrevocable.

I'm talking about your time, of course; and your talents, your passions, your money, your jobs, your dreams and plans: your stuff. But more than that, I'm talking about your heart and soul. Jesus seemed to think that if you love any of these things too much, if you cling to these things so tightly that you do not offer them freely to the world, then you may indeed have a life, for a time, but chances are you haven't really lived.

Jesus was not the only one in the New Testament to choose self-offering over self-preservation. Look at Paul, who left behind a brilliant, successful career at the synagogue in order to preach Christ to the Gentiles. Paul says, *I had it all, and I gave it all away that I might receive a far greater inheritance.* It was a choice that would ultimately lead to five public whippings, three beatings with rods, one public stoning, two shipwrecks, imprisonment, house arrest, and serious illness. But we are here today because of Paul's little seed. His grain of wheat grew a harvest, a legacy.

Look at the people in the very first church in the book of Acts, who, as Luke reports, sold everything they had for one common purpose—so that no one had need. That was the very first stewardship campaign in the history of the church, only their pledge was more than houses and fields and personal property—it was their hearts and souls. And in offering them, Luke says the number of men and women who were added to their community grew daily.

The seeds of our Christian ancestors have given us life; from their harvest we are fed daily. In one hand we hold the bread they left for us; in the other hand, we each of us hold our own seeds, which, if we dare plant them, will one day feed our children.

Such is the case with a man who walked away from a high-paying, successful, promising career seven years ago because he woke up one day and realized he loved his wife and two kids more than the job that kept him away from them. After eating from the Bread of Life, he chose to find another way to make a living that would provide him the time and space to make a life for his family. He planted a seed, he's building a legacy, and it has cost him something.

I think of David Hilfiker, a physician who left his private practice in Iowa fifteen years ago, sold his stuff, packed up his family, and moved to Washington, D.C. There, he began practicing what he calls "poverty medicine" in the inner city, healing poor people with medicine, love, and the grace of Christ. He is changing the world. His life is a seed. His harvest is one of righteousness and justice.

I know a young woman who, four years ago, responded to God's call in her life to become a nurse—to bind wounds, to care for the dying, to empty bedpans, and change soiled sheets. She left her accounting job, studied full-time for four years, made personal sacrifices in her life, putting everything else on hold in order to achieve her goal. She graduated from nursing school this year and now walks the halls of the local hospital, planting seeds, building a legacy—a harvest of compassion and healing.

I never knew the man who gave me my middle name, but I know his legacy. Sergeant Robert O'Bannon, 2nd Platoon, Echo Company, 2nd Battalion, 4th Marines—my uncle. Five years ago he was posthumously awarded the Silver Star, the highest honor for a Marine. In March 1968 he crossed heavily defended enemy lines to rescue a wounded soldier and a Naval medic who were trapped in the smoke, flying debris, screams, and explosions of an aborted mission. Five days later he was killed by a mortar round at Vinh Quan Thuong. His daughter, my cousin, inherited his legacy five years ago, when his story was finally told by the Naval medic whom he pulled from a crater and dragged to safety. That moment brought a necessary healing that marked the beginning of her journey toward sobriety. A seed planted over thirty years ago had finally broken the surface, and it looked like peace.

When you add it all up you discover that the legacy of these and other saints—both the living and the dead—is not about a single life at all, but one life, from which we all of us live. We are the wheat he has left behind; this church is the fertile soil of his field; the seeds we plant are our very hearts and souls; and the legacy that they produce points to Jesus Christ, who by his own free choosing showed us that self-offering, letting go, even death itself, is not so scary after all; who, in climbing up on the cross for us, showed us what is possible—life out of death, redemption out of self-offering, a harvest from a single seed, a legacy from a life.

Video Clip Suggestion

Life as a House (New Line Cinema, 2001)

Upon his diagnosis with terminal cancer, George makes some necessary changes in his life and builds his dream house, recruiting his estranged wife and children to assist him. "I always thought of myself as a house." he says at the end of the film. "That was always what I lived in. It didn't need to be big; it didn't even need to be beautiful; it just needed to be mine…I became what I was meant to be—I built myself a life, I built myself a house" (1:55:00—1:59:00).

Blessed Thorns

2 Corinthians 12:2–10

Therefore I am content with weaknesses, insults, hardships, persecutions, and calamities for the sake of Christ; for whenever I am weak, then I am strong. (2 Cor. 12:10)

I visited with Minnie Martin this week. She is unable to walk as a result of a stroke, which has paralyzed her right side. She is unable to speak now, communicating instead through written messages on a small green notepad in the handwriting of her old age. She is also unable to eat, and has recently made the conscious decision to forego surgery to insert a feeding tube that would prolong her life. We talked about that decision this week, but it was for her a brief conversation. Instead, she wanted to talk about how good God has been to her over her eighty-eight years of life, and how ready she is to inherit the Kingdom.

On her small green notepad, she wrote the following words, which I want to share with you—a statement of faith so profound and odd that it must be told. She wrote, "I can't walk. I can't eat. I can't talk." And then she wrote the most curious words of all—"God is blessing me." I paused for a moment to reflect on that progression of thought. "Can't walk, can't eat, can't talk. God is blessing me."

What Minnie was telling me on Thursday afternoon is that through the present suffering and struggles of her life, God is blessing her; she was telling me that these "thorns" of life, as the apostle Paul called them, have become the very evidence of God's love for her.

It's such a countercultural, counterintuitive thing to say, isn't it? It doesn't quite match up with what you and I are often told about faith—that when you believe in God and follow the narrow path of Jesus, you'll have fewer problems and more successes and your life will actually improve. You hear people attach the word *blessing* to *good* things, right? A good job, a healthy family, a close-call experience that turned out okay in the end, a promotion, a recovery from a terrible illness—these are all what we call "blessings" in this world. And maybe they are. It certainly feels like a blessing when God throws you a rope and pulls you through and it turns out that you actually don't have to suffer.

But what can we say about God when the rope does not appear? Can the terrors and hardships and heartbreaks and sufferings of life be blessings, too? I do not know anyone who would prefer this option, and I admit my reluctance to speak too quickly and freely about it, knowing that God may test me on it.

I am not saying I like the thought of that. I am human, after all, and I want God to do things my way too much of the time. Given the choice between the best case and the worst case scenarios in my life, between comfort and catastrophe, between the good and the not-so-good, I'm not embarrassed to tell God, "All things being equal, let me tell you which options I prefer."

The only problem is that God does not ask nearly as often as I think God should. That is why the apostle Paul's letter this morning is worth listening to. In this part of the letter, right here in 2 Corinthians 12, he talks about the worst-case scenarios he's been through—the awful things none of us would prefer, if given the choice; and reflecting on all of that, he concludes, like Minnie Martin, that God is blessing him.

Paul was a first-century church planter, but he never stayed in one church very long. He started churches, and once convinced that the church was strong enough to survive without him, he moved on to start another. He did not stay long in Corinth—maybe a year and a half or so; certain that the Corinthian church plant had taken root and was bearing much fruit, Paul set off for Ephesus to start all over.

While in Ephesus, Paul wrote the Corinthians a letter—now known as 1 Corinthians—in response to a letter the church had sent to him shortly after his departure. According to their letter to him, things were not going very well in his absence: Members were arguing, factions were dividing the body, and the metropolitan setting of Corinth brought all kinds of moral and behavioral challenges to the church. Paul addressed these issues in his first letter, but when he did not hear back from them he decided to send his personal emissary, Timothy, to drop in on the Corinthian church and assess the situation firsthand.

Timothy returned to Paul with news of serious problems, not the least of which was that a group of Jewish-Christian missionaries had arrived at Corinth and seemed to be undermining Paul's teaching and apostolic authority. In his second letter to Corinth, Paul refers to them as "super-apostles" and "Satan's ministers." These guys were apparently very compelling, by the way. They used big words that few could understand; they were very good looking and smarter than the average bear; they wore Armani suits and drove big cars and, we can only imagine, were already planning a global satellite television ministry.

Unlike Paul and the rest of the church he left behind, these super-Christians seemed to have it all together—and this was because they apparently had something spiritual that the rest of the church did not have, that Paul did not seem to have, but something that every good Christian leader needed, they said. What they had were "visions and revelations," of the secret mysteries of God, and they said that only those who were tight with God could get them, and that until you got them, you were not much of a Christian.

Maybe you have met Christians like this. They have seen something you have not seen. They have had some dramatic experience you have never had. Maybe they saw Jesus cooking in their kitchen in the middle of the night, or saw the face of the Virgin Mary in a flour tortilla; maybe they can speak in tongues, or they've seen the white light on the other side, or have had some out-of-body experience and lived to tell about it. Please do not misunderstand me. I am not making light of such experiences; in fact, I know many who have had them, whose lives have been changed by them, who have lived to tell about them with great conviction and passion. So please do not think I am passing judgment on such experiences. Paul certainly did not. But I will tell you what Paul said in his second letter to that church. Paul said that such experiences were not something to hang your hat on. The Christian life, this faith in Jesus, has little to do with how much you can say about the mysteries of heaven and the hidden things of God.

I know too many people who have told me over the years that they do not know why God has never given them a burning bush, or a dove with an olive branch in her beak, or a voice from a whirlwind, or a lighting bolt on the road to Damascus, or a parting sea. I know too many who expect this of God and are disappointed when they do not get it. And I also know too many people who get hung up on such experiences—people who have had them and never seem to get over themselves, who use them as justification for being heard, or respected, or followed.

"Nobody with a good car needs to be justified," said Hazel Motes in *Wise Blood*.[1] That was Flannery O'Connor's commentary on faith—anyone with a good "religious" experience never really seems to need the grace of Christ. At least one of these "super-Christians" told the Corinthian church that Paul was not the real deal, because Paul never talked much about those big revelations and visions. We do not know exactly how it was said, but we do know that it pained Paul when he heard about it. Maybe what he said was that Paul was as fragile as a clay jar; or that the persecutions Paul experienced were a disgrace to the community; or that he was a poor spokesman for God—always getting into trouble, doing jail time, getting beat up in public, or rubbing people the wrong way with his preaching (which was not always eloquent among the well-spoken Greeks). What he said, I think, was that Paul was making a joke out of the mysteries of God.

Paul could not argue about some of that. He *did* look a lot like Dennis the Menace with a Bible. Trouble seemed to follow him wherever he went, and he never tried to hide that fact. Unlike the "super-Christians," Paul looked *very* human, and very vulnerable.

But Paul felt the need to set the record straight with the Corinthians, writing a defense, which we just read this morning. He said, if it will help my cause, and win you back, I suppose I could boast of great things, too. I've had one of those visions everyone is talking about. *Once*. Fourteen years ago. It's been a while, I suppose, but I will always remember it. I was walking the dog one minute, and the next minute my head was poking through the clouds of the highest heaven, and yes, I could see the mysteries of God. It was very dramatic stuff. I heard things I cannot tell you—classified stuff. God said, "What you have seen and heard you cannot talk about." So I never did.

You can imagine that when people heard this, they were not too impressed. If you cannot talk about it, if you cannot tell us what you know of things up there, how do we know you're the real deal—how do we know you are truly blessed by God?

But Paul read their minds, and continued writing. He said, "If we're talking about blessings, then I can tell you all about that." Then he told them about this "thorn" in his life—not saying what it was, just that somewhere along his faith journey, he turned a corner in his life and some little thorn snagged him—stuck him in his side, so to speak, like a barbed treble hook, and he'd never been able to get rid of it, never been able to shake it. It was there every day. He used to pray that God would take it away, but God never did. Every time he prayed about it, God said, "No, I won't take this from you. Instead, my grace will have to be sufficient."

There has been a lot of talk about what that "thorn" in his life really might have been. Some say it was a physical ailment, or a speech impediment, or epilepsy, or partial blindness; some say it was a person in his life who gave him trouble. It could have been any number of things, as it can be today—a sour marriage, a child who will not go along with the family program, a job you do not like or a job you do not have, a tumor, depression, bankruptcy. Maybe you can't walk, can't talk, can't eat. What Paul said, however, is something so crazy that it has to be true. Paul said, "These are the *real* signs of God's presence and power in my life. Not visions or revelations, but this thorn that is there, everyday. When I get out of bed and make my coffee, it's there. When I get into the car and go to the office, it's there. When I go shopping, running, whatever—it's there. And it's reminding me that I have to depend on God's grace everyday; that I can't go it alone. I can't make it go away; instead, I have to turn to God, who gives me the strength everyday to live with it.

That is the kind of Christian I find most believable in this world—someone who will not keep his head stuck in his holy cloud too long; someone who is so grounded that he got snagged by a thorn on his way through life; someone who is so faithful that he will not seek any false means to have it removed. Paul believed this thorn was a means of grace in his life. He did not ask for it; he did not seek it out; he did not choose it. But it was his, and he was determined to transform it into a daily reminder of God's strength and goodness.

I do not know if this makes any sense at all, especially when that thorn is really digging deep and you're hurting, while everyone else seems to be climbing higher and higher into the clouds of life and calling it all a blessing. All I know is what Paul knew—that God's strength is made perfect in our weakness; that any effort to claim strength on our own, through visions or revelations or a life of perfection and success, only serves to steal the spotlight from God and shine it on ourselves. But our weakness is the holy stuff that God uses to reach us and strengthen us from within.

Anne Lamott writes about a ski trip she made with her friend, Sue Schuler, who was dying of cancer. It was Holy Week, and the passion story of Jesus became palpably real as Lamott observed her friend's own slow, painful journey. On Good Friday they celebrated holy communion together in a hotel room, and she later reflected on what it meant:

> It's such a sad day, all loss and cruelty, and all you have to go on is faith that the light shines in the darkness, and nothing, not death, not disease, not even the government, can overcome it. I hate that you can't prove it. If I were God, I'd have the answers at the end of the workbook, so you could check to see if you're on the right track, as you went. But nooooooo. Darkness is our context, and Easter's context: Without it, you couldn't see the light. Hope is not about proving anything. It's choosing to believe this one thing, that love is bigger than any grim bleak [crap] anyone can throw at us.
>
> After the Good Friday service, she wanted to show me her legs, the effects of all that skin grafting. The skin was sort of shocking, wounded and alien as snakeskin.
>
> "Wow." She let me study it awhile. "I have trouble with my cellulite," I said.
>
> "Yeah," she answered, "but this is what me being alive looks like now."[2]

Like I said, I understand very little of this, and I do not necessarily want God to test me on it, *ever*. But I do know that the thorns in my life, and the thorns that will surely snag me later, are proof of life. And I also know that in some strange, wonderful way, they are the one very real qualification for experiencing the grace of God, which is always sufficient in every weakness.

Video Clip Suggestion

About Schmidt (New Line Cinema, 2002)

(to illustrate how the people in our lives are blessed thorns)
Speaking at his daughter's wedding reception, Warren Schmidt finally accepts his new son-in-law, Randall, and Randall's eccentric extended family (1:47:00—1:53:00).

The Big Reveal

Luke 24:36–48

"Why are you frightened, and why do doubts arise in your hearts? Look at my hands and my feet; see that it is I myself. Touch me and see; for a ghost does not have flesh and bones as you see that I have." (Lk. 24:38–39)

Cynthia Audet grew up with a scar on her face. At the age of three she sustained an injury that left a perfect arrow on her cheek, pointing to her left eye. She was too young at the time to understand that facial scars were a bad thing, especially for a girl, she says. Growing up, she never seemed to mind the scar. In fact, she came to understand it as something that brought her attention and tenderness and candy.

As she grew older she began to take pride in her scar, in part to stop bullies from taunting her, but mainly to counter the assumption that she should feel embarrassed. Early on, she felt a certain embarrassment when people asked her about her scar. "What's that?" they asked. "What happened to you?" They called her "Scarface," but the more she heard how unfortunate her scar was, the more she found herself liking it.

When she turned fifteen her parents—on the advice of a plastic surgeon—decided that it was time to operate on what was by then a thick, shiny red scar. She protested. She told her parents that she didn't mind the scar, that she had come to like it, that she believed it made her even more pretty, unique, in her own special way. But her parents prevailed. "It's a deformity," they said. So the doctors operated—sanded down the arrow; and after a few surgeries, her cheek was smooth—the scar now visible only in the right light.

She is now in her late twenties, and she says she looks in the mirror with a certain sadness that the scar is no longer there. She says, "There was something powerful about my scar and the defiant, proud person I became because of it. I have never been quite so strong since they cut it out."[1]

I suppose that for some of you here, the notion that a scar can be a symbol, or a source of power, is unimaginable. We live in a culture of perfection, after all. We work hard to clean ourselves up, to look better, to appear younger than we are; and Madison Avenue works overtime to make us that way. Our appearance matters to us because we're told it matters to the world. The more perfect our image, the more powerful our identity. Our scars, our wounds, our visible deficiencies are perceived as weaknesses in this world. These tend to give us away; they do not lie. A war veteran amputee can convince you of the terrors of war without the use of words; a child bearing a purple bruise is questioned by her school counselor; track marks on a forearm point to a history of addiction; a white cane tapping the concrete will clear a crowded sidewalk. It is the not-so-perfect part of us that gets noticed in this world and points to the truth of who we are.

When the resurrected Jesus shows up and meets the disciples again for the first time, he discovers that convincing them that it is really him is far more difficult that walking out of the dark hole in the ground. Luke says they do not believe him. *It can't be Jesus. The real Jesus is dead. Dead as dead can be. We saw the cross, the tomb, the darkness, the death. Jesus is dead.* From what they can gather, what they see before them is not Jesus, but a ghost—the spirit of Jesus, but not the real thing. The real thing died three days ago, on the darkest day of their lives.

That is when Jesus steps toward them in that room in Jerusalem and says, "Look at my hands and my feet. Look at where the nails pierced my flesh. Touch it. Do ghosts have flesh and bones? Do ghosts have scars?"

According to Luke, the disciples were immediately filled with joy. They were still disbelieving; they had no rational explanation for what they were seeing with their very own eyes. But it gave them joy nonetheless. The scars of Jesus—his wounds—gave them joy. And that was enough to keep them from running away from what they could not yet understand.

It is strange, isn't it? His scars became his strength. His scars said something that no words, no rational explanation, no theory or doctrine or principle could possibly say. His scars said, "I am alive. I have survived the worst thing that could possibly happen to a person. My body has been pierced; my heart has been broken; I have been crushed in every way; I have been killed. And I have overcome it all. I am alive."

Try as we may to erase the scars and signs of our suffering in this world, Jesus shows us that these are the things that point to the truth of the resurrection—*our* resurrection. These are the compelling signs that announce to the world that suffering and hardship happens in this life of ours—it's unavoidable, inevitable, and real. Life is hard; we die little deaths everyday—through disappointments, through trials, through sin, through injustices of every kind. Suffering happens. But—and this is what Jesus proved to his disciples that day—God takes our suffering and makes it work for good in the world, to fulfill God's purposes, just as God took the suffering of Jesus and used it as a primary means of redemption. If that is true, then the scars we bear in our hearts and on our bodies can become sources of strength, evidence of God's power in the world, proof that the worst things can happen to you in this world and God is still faithful to raise you up out of it in order to bring joy to a disbelieving world.

I said earlier that some of you might not be able to grasp this. Perhaps it is a theological hurdle more than anything else. There is a strong thread of prosperity theology running through the fabric of Christian culture that says that suffering is *not* inevitable; it says that when you follow Jesus and commit your life to him, your life will get better, you will prosper, God will bless you richly. It says the more you give to God the more blessing you will get in return. Give God a nickel and he'll give you back a dime. The often unspoken assumption, of course, is that when tragedy strikes, when suffering visits your life, you have not done enough; or worse, you have done something *wrong*. Job, the great patron saint of suffering in the Old Testament, had a few friends who subscribed to this theory. "What did you do to deserve all of this suffering?" they asked him. "What you sow, you reap," they said, "so you must have sowed some bad seeds." This can be the worst suffering of all. When you apply that kind of theology to your own life, you see that the scars we bear from the suffering of life are signs of something that must be erased, or hidden, because they mark us as someone who has done wrong, or someone who's unredeemable.

Before our church changed addresses, back when we leased our storefront, I got to know our next-door neighbors, whose business was curiously named, "Outcast." How ironic is it that a business with the name "Outcast" moves in next to a church? The owner is now twenty-five years old. He sells clothes, mostly black T-shirts and studded-leather jackets and belts, to the young people in this town. Customers with mohawks and shaved heads walk though his doors all day, and I have met a few of them. You cannot talk with them without taking note of their extravagant body ornamentation—colorful tattoos on every square inch of body real estate, sterling silver piercings on every loose flap of skin. They are all marked with the signs and symbols of their unique experiences.

Some people drive beamers or build dream houses as symbols of what they deem important; our friends at Outcast choose to wear their symbols on permanent display.

And if you spend enough time with some of them, they will tell you that these symbols point to something in their life—to an experience, to a moment in their life, to a struggle, to suffering. What they are saying is: "Something has happened to me. Something has happened in my life that has marked me." Talk to anyone who has a tattoo, and that person will tell you a story about what it means, why he did it, what was going on in her life when she did it—the death of someone he loved; a new love; a broken relationship; a new beginning; an epiphany. These people mark those moments in their lives by marking their bodies, and it hurts, but that hurt often has a way of healing the deeper hurt in their lives. And they wear that symbol of suffering on the outside as an act of defiance against a world that says you must cover it up and make it go away. Not all tattoos serve this purpose, of course; but many do. These markings point to a kind of spiritual rite of passage, a baptism by fire, from which they have emerged stronger and more alive. As Marcel Proust once said, *"We are healed of a suffering only by experiencing it to the full."*² You can experience suffering to the full and still live. Jesus showed the disciples his own markings, his own piercings, and they believed. These markings became the symbols not of death, but of life. They were the evidence that he was one of them, that he suffered, but that his suffering did not defeat him.

After he shows them his scars, he tells them, "You are witnesses to these things." A witness is someone who speaks the truth of what has been seen—someone who will stand behind the experience of that truth even if it costs that person something dear. And here's the clincher: The Greek word Luke uses here means more than just that kind of witness; the word is *martys*, which means, literally, martyrs. Jesus was saying, "The scars I bear will be the scars you bear, and the scars that you will bear will be evidence of the truth I have proclaimed and evidenced in my own life and death and resurrection."

Your scars, your suffering, the trials that you endure and overcome, tell a profound story to the world about the resurrection of Christ in your life. And they have a way of giving hope, relief, and even joy to those who stare down the barrel of their own suffering. *You are witnesses to these things.* Your life can be a living, breathing gospel that honors Jesus and offers joy, just as Jesus gave joy to his disbelieving disciples.

When the surgeon told my father that his cancer was terminal, it felt like the wrecking ball had crashed through our little family. My father was forty-eight years old, with no more than six months to live. The surgeon suggested a radical surgery to remove portions of his esophagus and stomach and to re-plumb his digestive tract. The surgery would not cure him; it would simply buy him time—perhaps a few years—assuming that the surgery did not kill him first. The surgeon warned my father that this treatment would be more painful than the disease.

There was a man in that hospital, a stranger named Frank who helped my father make his decision. Frank was three months removed from the same surgery, and he dropped in on my father to encourage him to go through with it. He sat down next to my father's bed, talked about the surgery, the recovery, and, yes, even the horrors that he endured. Then he removed his shirt, revealing a scar that traveled from his chest to his navel and all the way around to his shoulder blade. The scar was terrifying, but the good man looked squarely into my father's eyes and said simply, "You can do this. You can do this."

"I only have so much time," writes David Eggers;

> I know that sounds ridiculous, I seem young, healthy, strong, but things happen, I know you may not think so, but things happen to me, to those around me, they truly do…so I need to grab this while I can…Oh please let me show this to millions. Let me be the lattice, the center of the lattice. Let me be the conduit. There are all these hearts, and mine is strong, and if there are—there are!—capillaries that bring blood to millions, that we are all of one body and that I am—Oh, I want to be the heart pumping blood to everyone… oh let me be the strong-beating heart that brings blood to everyone! I want—
> And that will heal you?
> Yes! Yes! Yes! Yes![3]

"Look at my hands, my feet," says Jesus. "Touch me. Feel my scars. You are witnesses to these things. You are my witnesses. You are my evidence, the lattice, the capillaries, the blood-pumping heart that brings life. You are. And that will heal you."

It Takes One to Know One

1 Corinthians 1:18–25

For the message about the cross is foolishness to those who are perishing, but to us who are being saved it is the power of God. (1 Cor. 1:18)

Sometime this week my inbox will be flooded with e-mails announcing this year's Darwin Awards. Have you heard of these? Every year, a few of you send me these e-mails. You can log on to www.darwinawards.com on April 1 to get the best stories of those who, as the Web site says, have "improved the human gene pool by removing themselves from it." Most of the awards are given posthumously, of course, which is why I do not recommend you try to make the list.

These are purported to be true stories of people doing stupid things, such as standing on a chair with wheels while cleaning a bird cage on a twenty-third story balcony (the chair moved, and the person tumbled down twenty-three stories), or rock climbers attempting to answer an incoming call on their cell phones from 7,000 feet up, or counterfeiters trying to pass off $16 bills at the local bank. My favorite all-time Darwin Award went to Lawn Chair Larry, as he is called, who, in 1981, fulfilled his life-long dream of flying by attaching forty-five weather balloons to his lawn chair. Did you hear about this one? He loaded up a couple of sandwiches, a six-pack of beer, and a pellet gun, and filled each 4-inch balloon with helium. Now, Larry had a plan, of course. He had anchored his chair to his Jeep with 30 feet of rope, and had planned to pop each balloon with his pellet gun when he was ready to descend. His friends, however, cut the rope as a prank just as he reached the end of his rope, so to speak, and Larry shot up into the sky like a rocket—first to 100 feet, then to 1000 feet, and eventually leveled off to an *un*comfortable cruising altitude of 16,000 feet, right over the flight path of LAX. By the time he popped each weather balloon with his pellet gun, Lawn Chair Larry ended up twenty miles from home, somewhere in Long Beach, entangled in power lines, where he was eventually rescued and immediately arrested. When asked later why he did it, Lawn Chair Larry replied, "Because a man can't just sit around."

Brilliant, isn't it? We all have a few of our own Darwin Awards, don't we? the foolish things we do in life that are better left untold? Most of us wouldn't make the Darwin list, of course, but we're all a bunch of fools, aren't we? The saving grace in it all is that, most of the time, the foolish things we do are done in private, where no one is there to see. You ever find yourself driving your car down the freeway and suddenly panicking because you can't find your keys? We are fools, aren't we? But most of the time, we are closet fools.

This leads me to ask the dangerous question this morning—what are we doing here? Why are we here, in church, setting aside an hour of our precious time worshiping a God who comes to Earth in flesh and blood—nothing foolish about that. But it's what this God named Jesus does that confounds us. He forsakes every sign and expression of worldly success and chooses to die a criminal's death on a cross staked to a trash heap outside of town, where his friends abandon him, where his adversaries mock him, where it even seems to some that God has left him all alone. "Where is your God now?" they ask.

It's crazy, when we really think about it. While none of us wants to be taken as a fool in this world, we have taken up a faith that is nothing short of foolishness, the way the world sees it. We are fools who gather to worship the King of Fools—Exhibit A of how *not* to be successful, believable, a winner.

It all starts off pretty reasonable and successful. You read any of the gospels—pick one, it doesn't really matter which one you read—and Jesus looks like a man destined for great things, great success. He is a miracle worker, turning water into wine, loaves and fishes into a humanitarian food drop in the desert. He heals the sick, the blind, the deaf, the lepers; he loves the children, the outcasts, the sinners no one else will love. He gives people hope, purpose, opportunity, and community. He draws a crowd every time he speaks. He is the next big thing, right?—a blessing to everyone he meets, regardless of where they come from, where they've been, who they are. It's a beautiful thing to believe in a God like this. It's not a stretch to believe in a guy like that.

But read on. Read every little pearl of wisdom he casts, every little parable, every teaching, and the man starts to look a little whacked out to rational, reasonable people like us.

"Blessed are the poor," he says. *Really? Since when is poverty a blessing? Would the woman on the corner with the "work for food" sign agree?* "Blessed are those who are persecuted." *With all due respect, Jesus, can you tell me what's so blessed about getting a noogie or a wedgie from the bullies in your life? Have you seen the dirty faces of those who hurt in this world, the blistered feet and bloated bellies of the world's refugees?* "Love those who curse you, pray for your abusers, turn the other cheek, and if someone steals from you, don't ask for it back." *Jesus obviously has never driven the 405 Freeway at rush hour, or lost his retirement fund to Enron, or his childhood innocence to the cruelty of angry men.* But he won't stop. "Do not fear those who kill the body; love your enemies; give away your possessions; don't worry about your life, what you will eat, or if you will ever find work or how you will retire or how you will put your kids through college." *Really? Jesus, this sounds absurd*. But still he will not stop. "He who does not hate his mother or his father, or his brothers or sisters, even his very life cannot follow me." *So much for family values*. "The greatest of all is servant of all." *Try that one at the office and see how far you get up the corporate ladder*. "If you look on another with lust, you have committed adultery in your heart." *Try that one at the mall, without a blindfold*. "If your eye causes you to sin, cut it out; your hand, cut it off." *Really?* It all sounds interesting on paper, of course, but I do not see anyone here wearing eye patches or prostheses from practicing such noble disciplines. He just won't stop. It's everywhere in the gospels. "Lose yourself to find yourself, take up your cross, if you want to follow me, give up your life." These are not footnotes to his teachings; these *are* his teachings. Am I the only one here who finds this stuff utterly foolish? The disciples did. "If this is what it's all about, Jesus," they said, "then who can be saved? *Who* can do this? *Who?"*

We start out following Jesus in order to cook up a little chicken soup for the soul, you know? Something warm and inspiring and reasonable; something that goes down easy and satisfies. What we get is a splintered, terrifying cross that seems impossible, and so unnecessary.

Which means that we are indeed either fools, or hypocrites, sitting here today. Or perhaps, by the grace of God, a little of both. It seems so hard, because it is. But Christians are those who refuse to edit out of the story the incredible challenge of faith. They understand that the way of Jesus is hard to achieve.

Some do not understand this. They take the more palatable teachings of Jesus, mix them in with a little from Buddha and Gandhi and Leo Buscaglia, stir in a little Steven Covey and Muhammad and a tablespoon of family values, and bake it into a pretty manageable, reasonable, safe way of life. And don't get me wrong—you can get a pretty good life by doing that. You will never hear me say that such a life is wrong; I will not make that judgment. You can get a very safe, centered, inner-peace kind of life by taking all the best of what you like from the best of who you know and coming up with a way that works best for you. Paul just wanted you to know that you cannot get Christ by doing that.

And I know what Paul meant, because if it were left to us, we would get all of that good stuff without the cross, without the suffering, without the foolish, seemingly unnecessary danger and sacrifice that comes from following such a God. Paul said, I can't preach anything but the cross, because the cross says something particular about God that no worldly philosophy can, and it makes me a particular kind of person—odd, foolish, perhaps; but real. The cross says that the road to abundant life is hard and narrow and long and sometimes terrifying. The cross says that there are times when you cannot take the best of everything in general and still stand for something in particular. The cross says that in life we will have to make some hard choices—to go one way or the other, to say yes or to say no, to forsake even flesh and blood for spirit and truth. Paul wanted people to know that Christianity was not like any other religion or philosophy. Christianity has this cross, which for some is the way that leads to an abundant but risk-taking life, and for others is the stumbling block they just cannot get around.

But Paul says it cannot be removed, because it is the lens through which we see the world and our lives, and the rule by which we live and breathe and have our being. It is a stumbling block because it reminds us that faith is a sacrifice, a constant letting go of everything that makes us just like everyone else in order to be made into something holy, odd, distinctive, set apart. Does that mean that it makes us better than everyone else? I hope not. The cross is not a throne that elevates us over others; its power tends to have the opposite effect, stripping us clean of our crowns and dressing us with a mantle of humility and sacrifice.

I met with a remarkable man a few months ago who cracked his shin on this stumbling block. He is twenty-eight years old, well-educated, good-looking. And he is someone who is trying very hard to take his Christian faith seriously.

He had been engaged to a very beautiful young woman—the complete package, you know: brains, beauty, fashion, and style. She was not a Christian, and she made it clear that she did not want to go there, did not want to share that part of his life with him. It was a stumbling block for her; she would not get around it. So he came in to ask me what I thought of that, even though I am not his pastor. He knew his Bible, especially the part that warns of being unequally yoked in our relationships. We talked about what that meant for him; we also talked about the unique challenges of marriage and his own clear sense of Christian vocation. We talked it through, we prayed together, and he agreed to wait on God for the answer.

A month later he wrote me a letter in which he shared that he had broken off the engagement and the relationship, that the pain and sadness of that decision brought also a sense of relief and freedom. He wrote, "For the first time in my life, I know that following Christ can break your heart."

"For the message of the cross is foolishness to those who are perishing, but to us who are being saved it is the power of God." Paul wants us to know that this cross will either be a stumbling block that keeps us from the kingdom of Heaven, or the very power of God that will save us and show us a way in. We will either let our *"outside tide us over 'till our time runs out,"* as Harry Chapin once sang,[1] or we will live from the inside, where that strange, odd, foolish power of the cross pulses and pounds and drives us deeper into the heart of God, deeper into the Kingdom.

Clarence Jordan was a Southern Baptist preacher who, in the 1940s, founded an interracial community in Americus, Georgia, called Koinonia Farm. Advocating for civil rights at that time, in that place, was risky business. There were bomb threats; there were threats on Jordan's life. But he remained committed to the odd, dangerous cross of Jesus. Jordan had a brother, a lawyer and aspiring politician, to whom he went for legal help in the face of this ongoing persecution. His brother refused to get involved with Koinonia for fear of risking his promising political career. One day Clarence Jordan told his brother that he should go back to that little church where they had once walked down the aisle to commit their life to Christ and explain something to the people there. He said, "Go tell them that what you really meant to say was that you *admire* Jesus, not that you want to *follow* him."[2]

Do not be misinformed. The day you choose to follow Jesus is the day your trouble starts. There will be occasions when you will have to stand up and speak out when your instincts tell you to remain silent. Opportunities will arise when you will have to step out on a limb for something you believe in, even when the chainsaw is set to the tree. Like Paul, you may have to stand up and tell the truth about who you are to people who will immediately mock you for it, or judge you for it. Like Jesus, you may have to open a vein to bleed for something that cries out for a transfusion of life, of grace, of love.

It takes one to know one, they say, and the day you take up whatever cross Jesus gives you is the day you know him most fully. But that, of course, requires some strange, odd, foolish living in the time that we still have. It requires some dying to the things that *tide us over*—some shedding, some peeling away of the outside, and some raising of this thing inside us that our life has yet to be about, this cross, this odd, strange foolish cross—this wisdom and power of God.

PART 3

Transformation

It is widely understood that the young Christians who occupy our churches these days are decidedly pragmatic in their theology and politics, and highly suspicious of universal claims, sweeping social agendas, consensus and conformity, institutions and ideologies. The Social Gospel that captured the imagination of Boomers in the 60s and 70s has been broadly rejected by Generation Xers in favor of a more local, deeply personal theology of liberation. Motivated by the flesh-and-blood loyalties of family, tribe, community, and friends, they cast a skeptical eye on abstract theories, bloated institutions, big government, and political promises, which have most often let them down. Xers seek to fix only what seems to be fixable, beginning with their own mess and moving out to what is tangible, reachable, touchable, and local.

This does not suggest that Xers are disinterested in the transformation of the world. It means, rather, that they are more likely to volunteer at a soup kitchen than march on Washington for the rights of the poor. They'll participate at the local beach clean-up, but likely will not attend a workshop on global warming. And they will give their time, money, and resources—to the church, to movements, to political parties—on the basis of personal principle and values, not institutional duty or loyalty.

This pragmatism rings true for Xers with respect to their sense of personal, spiritual transformation as well. Broad, sweeping, immediate transformation/conversion is regarded suspiciously, often perceived as a consequence of religious coercion, manipulation, and conformity.

The *journey* is valued over the *destination*; along the way, all things are made new, one at a time. Money, time, commitments, relationships become sacramentals—ordinary means by which we both receive and share the grace of God—that empower and sustain us along the way.

The sermons in this unit seek to turn the gaze of the listener inward to consider the ways in which we are constantly being pulled into the current of conformity in this world, and to name our unique Christian identity as odd and subversive; to consider the time of our lives as a resource that demands faithful stewardship of it; to reflect on what it means to persevere on our faith journey in a culture that places a premium on feelings and emotion; and finally, to address the issue of the stewardship of money as means of declaring our freedom in this world. By beginning with the inward, honest gaze, we are called to become the kind of change we want to see in the world, and are equipped to act on it in practical, meaningful ways.

Home Alone

Luke 2:41–52

"Child, why have you treated us like this?" (Lk. 2:48)

Have you ever noticed that Jesus just doesn't fit in? Doesn't matter where he is, Jesus just doesn't fit in. The holy family is on the road home from Jerusalem. They loaded up the Winnebago, dropped into formation in the long caravan of holiday travelers on the 91 Freeway, and began their slow journey home. It was a sea of cars, bumper to bumper the whole time, touch and go, touch and go. They got about halfway home, a full day's journey, when Joe looks at Mary and says, "You know, Jesus is awfully quiet back there. Jesus, you okay back there? Jesus?"

It was the day Jesus got left behind, but part of me wonders if he was *ever* with them, even when he was with them. You think it's tough being a parent these days—just try being a parent of the Savior of the world. Keeping an eye on him constantly, making sure he's keeping his nose clean, keeping his grades up; making sure he carried out his chores. How do you discipline the Messiah, for heaven's sake? You try to come down hard on him and he just looks at you and says, as Robin Williams puts it, "You're not my real dad."[1]

If you are Mary and Joe, you want to do everything in your power to keep things normal in his life. No special treatment, no excuses. You want your son to fit right in, right? You want him to conform to the same standards every other son in the neighborhood has to live by. *Jesus, be a good family boy, follow the rules, take it easy on Mom and Dad*. But one day he comes up missing. Not a word before he left. He didn't leave any clues behind. Just gone.

It was the start of a pattern for Jesus. He would never conform to your expectations. He didn't fit into his family's expectations, says Luke this morning. But he didn't fit into *anything*. When he became an adult, he didn't fit into his religion—in fact, they ran him right out of the temple with stones in their hands. He didn't fit into society—he was, after all, a carpenter's boy, born of Jewish peasantry, who hobnobbed—not with the in-crowd, the wealthy, the powerful—but with prostitutes, tax collectors, Gentiles, and Samaritans. Whenever he preached, his sermons didn't fit the expectations of those who would ordain him to preach—"Blessed are the poor, the weak, the mourning, and *woe* to you who are rich, powerful, and happy." What's that about? Jesus didn't fit in. Born the Savior of the world—and laid in a *manger*, a splintered feed trough, next to a pile of fresh manure in a forgotten place called Bethlehem. Didn't fit in. Claimed to be the Messiah, yet hung on a cross mounted atop a garbage heap next to two criminals at a place called Golgotha. Didn't fit in. From the cradle to the grave, and all points in between, Jesus didn't fit in.

He lived a life that some probably call lonely. All the mothers would talk when Mary wasn't around. "Have you seen that boy Jesus?" they'd say. "Mary's boy? Yeah, I've seen him. Seems a bit odd, doesn't he?"

All the kids are out riding their Razors™ and playing roller hockey in the street, and there's Jesus, sneaking off to the temple to learn scripture, to ask the rabbis questions. That's weird. Twelve years old? That's strange. Jesus never fit in.

And yet we follow him, which makes us more than just a little strange, I think, because part of making it in this life, part of becoming successful and claiming a name for ourselves in this culture has everything to do with fitting in, being accepted, being acceptable. If you want to climb the corporate ladder, conform, toe the company line. If you want to win the election, conform to the party, build bridges, follow the polls. If you want to get into the right college, or find your soulmate, or land the right job, then by all means, look normal, right? Fit in. Be like everyone else, just do it a little better. Mainstream. Middle of the road. Conform.

"Everybody I know," said TV producer Norman Lear, "drinks the right beer when they ain't sippin' the right soft drink; they're using the right deodorant and rinsin' with the right conditioner." Fitting right in. I remember going to a Christian concert when I was ten. I was too young at the time to know that "Christian concert" was code for "crusade." I sat up near the front. The musician played for about an hour, then he put down his guitar and told his story. "Used to be a mess," he said. "Used to sing in a band. All the drugs, booze, and women—I had it all. Then I found Jesus, and gave my life to him." And then he said that I could do that too, because I was a mess just like he once was. So he gave an altar call and invited us to turn our lives over to Jesus. And all these poor wrecks went up and did it. But I just sat there. I think I must have been the only one in the audience that just sat there. Even my best friend went up there, and I was *appalled*. I *knew* about him. He was twelve. He had never touched drugs; I never once saw him drink a single beer; he didn't know the first thing about sex. What is he doing? I was ten, for heaven's sake. There was no way I was going up on that stage like everyone else. Besides that, I was Catholic, and my mom would ground me if I even thought about it. Everyone, it seemed, got "saved" that night, except for me. I was the odd one who failed to go with the flow, and for the first time in my life I felt the awkward loneliness of not being part of the crowd, of not conforming to the expectations of those who seemed to know what was best for me.

We are born into the river of conformity to such a degree that to go against the flow is to be considered different. It also leads to a lot of alienation and persecution in this world. Dare to be odd, and you will likely pay the price for it.

I remember counseling with a man who had just lost his job. His partners had crossed some serious ethical boundaries in their business practices; they were both alcoholics; one was unfaithful to his wife and the other was dangerously close. So the man confronted them, offered to help them make things right and get square and come clean and start fresh. Perfect love casts out all fear, right? He went home that night, and when he returned to the office the following day, security met him at the front door with an empty box. There is a price to be paid for not conforming.

"Do not be conformed to this world," says the apostle Paul, "but be *transformed* by the renewing of your minds" (Rom. 12:2). That's what Jesus was doing in the temple when he turned up missing; that's what Jesus did his whole life. But how do you do that? How do you find the kind of peace within yourself to stand against the tide? How do you find the courage to go against the flow, to resist conforming to the ways of the world, especially when it costs you something the world deems valuable?

Paul said, "I appeal to you…by the mercies of God, to present your bodies as a living sacrifice, holy and acceptable to God" (Rom. 12:1). Isn't that what Jesus did? Jesus understood that his entire life was an offering to God—everything he did was replete with holy significance; every word he spoke was a word that God overheard. Jesus knew that. I think that is why he said to his mother, "Why didn't you know I would be in my Father's house?" Even at the age of twelve, he seemed to understand that his life belonged to God. It all started there in the temple that day, but that was just the beginning. Look how it grew from there. Every life he touched—it was God moving through him. Every moment was a God moment, infused with divine opportunity. Every journey he took—it wasn't just about getting to the destination, it was about attending to the Spirit's leading at every turn. His whole life was given to the work of God.

We, on the other hand, divide up what we think belongs to God and what we think belongs to us. We get this confused. We start to think that an offering is simply what we give on Sunday; that spiritual things belong at church, and the rest of our life is free to do with as we choose.

Paul says you are an offering to God, and every day that offering plate is passed right before you. *Every day*. What are you going to put in that plate today? Not just here at church. That is not what makes you different. Not just today, not just here and now; but tomorrow, out there, in the world, what will you offer?

Sacramentalize everything you can in this world. Make everything a means of grace, make every moment an opportunity for pleasing God. Make every deed, every word, every thought a fragrant offering to God. Understand that every word is heard by God, every deed seen by God, every thought known by God, who knows every secret hidden in the heart. This is the only cure for cultural conformity that I know of, and I do believe it is a good one.

Maybe that means that when we sit in front of our bowl of cereal, we see a holy meal, a sacrament, just as Jesus made a sacrament out of the ordinary gifts of bread and wine. Maybe that means that when we play board games with our children, we will remember that even this is an offering pleasing to God. Maybe that means that when we meet a stranger, we know we might be entertaining angels in welcoming him. Maybe that means that when we experience hardship or disappointment or failure, we do not ask, "Why me?" but rather, "Where is God in this?" Every moment, every act—these are the daily offerings we drop in that plate to remind us how odd we truly are in Christ.

The story of Rosa Parks is a familiar one. On Thursday, December 1, 1955, in Montgomery, Alabama, Parks left work and boarded the bus on Cleveland Avenue to go home. She didn't look at the bus driver when she boarded the bus; if she had she would never have ridden that bus, she says. After depositing her fare she looked up and saw that the driver was James Blake, who twelve years earlier had removed her from his bus for not following segregation laws. Whenever she saw a bus driver whom she knew to be mean, she refused to ride that bus.

But on that day it was too late. She sat down in the front seat of the black section of the bus. As the bus made its rounds white people filled the bus until there were no more seats in the white section. A white man got on and walked back to where Parks was sitting, and the bus driver told the people sitting in the front row of the black section to leave their seats. The man beside Parks moved out of his seat. The two women across the aisle from her rose and gave up their seats. Parks slid across her seat and sat next to the window. When the angry bus driver came back and told her to get out of her seat, she refused. "Well," he retorted, "I'm going to have you arrested." "You may do that," Parks answered.

In an interview a few years ago, Rosa Parks clarified a key misconception about that event: "People always say that I didn't give up my seat because I was tired, but that isn't true. I was not tired physically…No, the only tired I was, was tired of giving in."[2]

Rosa Parks refused to conform, to go with the flow. She made her protest a spiritual protest, and she made her life a holy offering.

She has become widely recognized by historians of the civil rights movement as a symbol for freedom and human rights.

We are all symbols—peculiar, different, odd, strange. Jesus makes us so. There is no way to follow Jesus without finding ourselves standing in the middle of the current while the rest of the fish head downstream. There is often a price to be paid for that, but even more, there is an incredible inheritance waiting for us when we do.

The explorer Cabeza de Vaca kept a journal in which he recorded the journey he and a fellow traveler had made from Florida to the Pacific in the early sixteenth century. In the journal he wrote about how the native Americans would come to them and ask them to heal the sick. The two explorers were themselves half starved and sick and filled with despair from having been away from their homeland for so long. But the natives believed that these explorers were gods, filled with divine power to heal the sick, and that they could heal if only they chose to do so. Although de Vaca felt that neither of them had such power, he wrote in his journal, "We had better do something or die. So we prayed for strength. We prayed on bended knee and in the agony of our need." One night they blessed the ailing natives; and to their amazement, on the following morning, they perceived that the sick had been healed. In his journal, de Vaca writes these words, "We were more than we thought we were."[3]

We are more than we have become. We are symbols, every last one of us—a living, breathing, walking sacrifice, holy and acceptable to God. And when the offering plate is passed, we would do well to climb right in.

Keepers of the Flame

Matthew 25:1–13

"The bridegroom came, and those who were ready went with him into the wedding banquet; and the door was shut."
(Mt. 25:10)

I have this recurring dream as a preacher. I talk to other preachers from time to time who tell me they have similar dreams. Preachers who do not have next Sunday's sermon germinating in their head by Tuesday night should not dare to fall asleep. You get these terrible, panic-stricken dreams in which you find yourself half-clothed in the pulpit on Sunday morning, or realizing that your lips have been sewn shut by the high school youth group, or looking down at your sermon manuscript only to discover that it's been written in Sanskrit.

Deep down we know that time is never on our side, though we tend to live as if it is. The *urgent* often claims the lion's share of our attention, while the *necessary* seems almost always to wait until the eleventh hour. Our lives are an endless, creative game of putting off and catching up, pushing back and pulling in, killing time and buying time. As the sun sets and darkness falls on another day of our lives, we make the bold assumption that tomorrow will always come, and rarely are we surprised that it does.

How much time do we have to do what must be done in our lives? Jesus said we have enough. He said we have more than enough time. But he also said it's what we do, or don't do, with the time we are given that becomes our greatest obstacle to the extraordinary inheritance of the kingdom of God.

He tells this story on what we know was one of his last few days of life. When you're terminal, so to speak, when you know your days are numbered, you cut to the chase and tell it like it is; you say what must be said, even if it hurts, because there may not be another opportunity in which to say it. And it's that sense of urgency, I suppose, that makes this such a hard word to hear and so seemingly contrary to the gospel of grace that dominates our perception of Jesus. The door to the Kingdom seems always to be open: Prodigals are welcomed home, the lost sheep are sought out and brought back into the fold, sinners find forgiveness, even tax collectors and prostitutes are given a place at the table. We fall in love with a Jesus who is patient and long-suffering, who waits and waits and seems to give us all the time we need to get it right and finally come around.

Then he broadsides us with a parable about the door slamming shut before we can squeeze through the threshold, and we discover that the grace of God apparently has a conscience. Matthew wields this story like cattle prod for his community of faith whose love for Christ had grown cold, whose light had begun to fade. Maybe Matthew saw his people going through the motions while quietly wondering if Jesus would ever return for them, as he promised them he would. It had been more than seventy years since that promise, and there was still no sign of his imminent homecoming. Maybe they were tired of waiting; maybe they were skeptical; maybe they were afraid that Nero's scouts would sniff them out and feed them to the lions or saw them in two. Whatever the problem was, Matthew felt it was time to tell them a little story that Jesus told his disciples three days before he was crucified, hoping to rekindle in them the flames of faith and inspire them to keep alert, to stay awake, to continue doing the work Jesus left for them to do.

It was not a *Chicken Soup for the Soul* kind of story, by the way. It was, rather, a terrifying story about ten bridesmaids who grab their lamps and head out to the roadside, waiting for the bridegroom to pull up in the limo for the wedding party. All ten show up. All ten wait. And wait. And wait. They have not heard the news that the limo hit a detour on the 5 Freeway. They haven't heard that the bridegroom is going to be late. The sun sets and darkness falls; the bridesmaids light their lamps, all ten of them, and they wait. But in their waiting, five of them notice that their lamps are running out of oil. Their light begins to flicker and fade, and before they know it, their lamps go out.

Curiously, at about that same time, the limo driver picks up his cell phone and calls the banquet hall, saying, "We're on our way; be there in a few." Word gets out, and the five bridesmaids panic; they are fresh out of oil, and a burning lamp is their only ticket to the party. The burnouts plead with the others—"share some of your oil with us, we didn't have time to stop and refuel on our way over." But there's not enough to go around. "Stuff's not cheap," the others say. "Only brought enough to get in." So the five burnouts climb into the minivan and head for the market, right about the same time the limo pulls around the corner and stops in front of the banquet hall. The five remaining bridesmaids, the ones whose lamps are still lit, escort the bridegroom to the entrance. The door opens. They walk through. The door shuts. And the party begins. It's living *la vida loca* in there, right? But no one inside could hear the five bridesmaids banging on the door in the dark night, pleading for a way in.

It is a hard story, but a necessary one, to be sure. We are apt to live our lives in this world as if there is always time to get around to doing what must be done now. Rarely do we ever pause to consider that our lives will someday come to an end, and all that we had planned on doing *someday* will have to be left undone. We set goals; we map out long-term plans; we work hard in order to retire comfortably someday. And if we do not get around to it all today, there is always tomorrow. For the average person, there are more than 26,000 tomorrows in a single lifetime. Plenty of time, right? If we don't get around to it today, there is always tomorrow, or the next day. But after reading the parable, I am not so sure about that.

Noah's neighbors laughed at the old man for hammering nails into planks of cypress and building a boat when the dark storm clouds gathered on the horizon. God would not hold back the rain for them. There was no tomorrow.

One day Jesus sent out the disciples to preach and teach and baptize, giving them specific instructions: *"If the people will not listen, if they reject you and refuse to let you in, then shake the dust off your feet, and move on."* God would not wait. The invitation was revoked.

When the rich man asked Jesus what he must do to inherit eternal life, Jesus told him straight up—"Sell all that you have, give it to the poor, and follow me." When the rich man turned and walked away grieving, Jesus did not negotiate a more pleasant deal, nor would he wait for the man to change his mind. The game clock had expired.

Go to a nursing home, or a cemetery, or a high school reunion, or a plastic surgeon if that is your thing, and you begin to see how many tomorrows have ticked off the clock of life, and how few tomorrows remain. "We turn faster than disks on a harrow," writes Annie Dillard, "than blades on a reaper. Time: You can't chock the wheels. We sprout, ripen, fall, and roll under the turf again at a stroke. Surely, the people is grass."[1] The doctor sees a spot on the CT scan; your best friend dies of a sudden heart attack at the office; planes dive headlong into office buildings in the New York skyline; a mushroom cloud thunders over the distant horizon. If you listen honestly, carefully, you can hear the door closing on the living all around us, and you take inventory of the oil you've been burning in your life, and the oil you've been banking.

As the hit musical, *RENT*, proclaims, "*There's no other road, no other way, no day but today.*"[2] There will not always be tomorrow. Jesus was clear about that. Life begins and life ends. There will be a day for all of us when the train will pull into the station. Jesus said, "Of that day or hour, no one knows." You're either prepared, or you're not. And he said that those who are wise are those who understand that you cannot make up for lost time.

Take a hard look at your spiritual dipsticks. Check to see how much oil you really have. Be honest about that, because when we are honest, I believe we will all of us discover that we are burning faith on old oil reserves that will some day run dry if we have not taken the time to draw deeply from the well of the One who promises to refill them.

I have heard too many people tell me over the years that they do not know why their adult children will not speak to them anymore. *If only I could go back and do what I put off over the years.* I have heard too many people tell me that they have spent their entire lives going to church and still do not know how to pray, or trust, or forgive, or love, or rest. I have sat with too many people over the years who, in the last days of life, confess that if they could do it all over again, they would slow down; give more and take less; be more generous with their love, their talents, their passions. They would store up more treasures in heaven and fewer possessions on earth. They would live the lives they've been given, rather than the many lives they've pursued in vain.

Jesus told the people one day on the mountain, "Do not worry about tomorrow—what you will eat or drink, what you will wear, what you will accomplish, who you hope to be, or what you hope to do someday. Worry instead about today. Let today's concerns be enough." Or, as Kathleen Norris says, "Live each day knowing that it may be your last. Someday you'll be right."

The Grapes of Wrath is John Steinbeck's powerful, epic story of the brutal circumstances of life in the days of the Dust Bowl in the 1930s, when an estimated 200,000 people fled their drought-ravaged homesteads for the promised land of California—many of whom never made it. The Joads pack their most essential possessions on the rear bed of their fragile jalopy, load up their family of twelve and the faithless preacher, and leave their home in Oklahoma in pursuit of a land of dreams too good to be true. As they head out of town into an uncertain, tragic future, Steinbeck gives us a glimpse of what it means to take each day, each moment as it comes:

> Al steered with one hand and put the other on the vibrating gear-shaft lever. He had difficulty in speaking. His mouth formed the words silently before he said them aloud. "Ma—" She looked slowly around at him, her head swaying a little with the car's motion. "Ma, you scared a goin'? You scared a goin' to a new place?"
>
> Her eyes grew thoughtful and soft. "A little," she said. "Only it ain't like scared so much. I'm jus' settin' here waitin'. When somepin' happens that I got to do somepin—I'll do it."
>
> "Ain't you thinkin' what's it gonna be like when we get there? Ain't you scared it won't be nice like we thought?"
>
> "No," she said quickly. "No, I ain't. You can't do that. I can't do that. It's too much—livin' too many lives. Up ahead they's a thousan' lives we might live, but when it comes, it'll on'y be one. If I go ahead on all of 'em, it's too much."[3]

There is considerable wisdom in that. Of all the lives ahead of us, only one of them counts—the one we're living today. That is all we can live. We cannot do more than that. Tomorrow may come. It might not. But today is here. And today is the day we are given to prepare for whatever tomorrow will bring, if indeed it comes at all. It is the oil we store up today that will keep the lights on tomorrow, in the kingdoms of this world, or in the Kingdom still to come.

Do not miss that Kingdom. Be keepers of the flame. Tend to the flame of Christ within you. Keep awake, keep alert, and let your light so shine before others that they might see your good works and give glory to the Father.

Video Clip Suggestion

About Schmidt (New Line Cinema, 2002)

Warren Schmidt has a moment of epiphany as he considers how much time he has left on the clock. Grieving the loss of his wife and his career, he determines that life is too short, that he cannot afford to waste another minute. Two weeks later, he wakes up in the same exact position without having made any changes in his life (0:43:00—0:44:00).

Born to Run
All-Saint's Day

Hebrews 12:1–2

Let us also lay aside every weight and the sin that clings so closely, and let us run with perseverance the race that is set before us, looking to Jesus the pioneer and perfecter of our faith. (Heb. 12:1b–2a)

A week after my father died in 1996, I helped my mother go through some of his things. We started in the garage, because that is where he spent so much of his time. That garage was holy ground; his workbench was an altar to the tool gods. Over the years we would sit there at that workbench and fix things—repairing bikes and tuning cars and restoring furniture. It was like a classroom, that garage. Everything I ever learned that really mattered, I learned right there in the garage. I still remember the day we had that father-son *facts of life* talk. I was in the family room watching a very provocative Prince video on MTV when my father said, "Son, time to have a little talk." I followed him out to the garage, took a seat at the workbench, and listened to him tell me everything I already knew.

From the garage, my mom and I went into his closet and sifted through suits and ties and hats and the leather belts with which I had become well acquainted in my early life. I remember looking down at the floor, right along the base of the wall, where all of my father's shoes were lined up in perfect formation like birds on a wire—leather shoes, tennis shoes, dress shoes, work shoes, sandals. Looking down at those shoes, I discovered something that I had never known about my father. I discovered that he never untied his shoes. The laces on every pair of shoes in that closet were still neatly tied in perfect bows. My father died with his shoestrings still tied, as if they still had some walking to do, as if there was still some place to go, some trail to blaze, some journey yet unfinished.

I looked once and saw a dozen pair of shoes with strings still tied. But I looked twice and saw the evidence of what it means to live as one who is always prepared to die, and to die as one who goes forth to live. Those shoestrings remained tied because my father was determined to keep going, to stay in the game, to get up the next day and do a little more, go a little farther, take a few more steps toward tomorrow.

There is a pretty good chance that someday we are going to die. The evidence is still fairly convincing. There is also a pretty good chance that we will most likely not be ready for it. It will likely come sooner than we expect, and it will likely leave us with some unfinished task. We will slip off our shoes at the end of the day and expect to slip them back on in the morning. But the morning will not come, and we will leave not only some unfinished task but also an unfinished life. There is both considerable challenge and grace in that fact—challenge to work with God to finish what has been started in our lives, to persevere at this task of living and believing for the time that we are given; and grace to accept that not all of it will get done.

That is why the author of Hebrews says, "We are surrounded by so great a cloud of witnesses,... [so] let us run with perseverance the race that is set before us." And you ask, "What cloud of witnesses?" Look at chapter 11, the chapter we did not read this morning. The author lists dozens of superheroes of the faith—Noah, Abraham, Sarah, Isaac, Jacob, Moses, David, Rahab, and Samuel, to name just a few. These are the big guns of the faith, right? These are the ones who ran the race of faith and took home the gold. It is like reading a list from God's hall of fame.

Then there is you, and me—who, by the way, will be hard-pressed to make that list. Sometimes it feels like we are not even in the same league, that the only way to get into that stadium is to buy a ticket and sit in the stands. Few of us will ever be called by God to lead an entire nation out of the Egypts of the world, as Moses was called to do, or to part the waters of a sea, or build an ark, or slay a Philistine giant; fewer still will ever risk being stoned to death or sawed in two for the sake of the gospel. No, it would seem that we are not even in the race when we stack ourselves up against these giants of the faith.

But the author of Hebrews thinks otherwise. This is what he says—"You are now surrounded by these saints. They have taken their turn around the track; they have carried the baton; they have endured the pain of the race—the burning legs, the breathlessness, the blisters in the feet, the pounding heart—and this is what they have done: They have passed the baton to you, and they've stepped off the track. They have taken a seat in the stadium to watch you run, to watch you take your laps on the track."[1] They did not go to the locker room for a hot shower, or to a place on the podium; they are here, all around us, and if you listen carefully you can hear them cheering you on, pulling for you, holding their breath when you stumble, willing you to get back up and stay in the race. Why? Because the race is not yet finished, not even for them. Their shoestrings are still tied because the race is not over until every last one of us crosses the finish line and the kingdom of God finally comes.

The author of Hebrews says that we are not running alone in this life. Maybe you wish you were. Maybe the thought of all the saints in heaven watching you, cheering for you, pulling for you—maybe that feels a bit intimidating to you. All I know is that we do need them, that we cannot run for very long without them, and Hebrews says they are here because they know what is on the other side of that finish line, and they want us to get across it.

When I ran cross country in high school, my parents would show up to the races and wait for me at the last half-mile. My mom would wear tennis shoes so that she could run with me and cheer me on when I came around the final stretch—embarrassing stuff when you're a high school senior. I would run faster just to drop her. But it was grace, too. It got me across that line, every time. Her shoestrings were always tied.

"We are surrounded by so great a cloud of witnesses, let us also lay aside every weight and the sin that clings so closely, and let us run with

perseverance the race that is set before us." Every obstacle in your life—get rid of it. Every hindrance, shed it; every ball and chain, cut it loose. You cannot run with that stuff. This is a race. Lighten the load.

I go into the bike shop every so often. I am a cyclist, and every cyclist wants the lightest bike: titanium frames; carbon fiber wheel sets; narrow seats that are so small it feels like you're riding on a seat post. Every serious cyclist wants to buy this stuff. I walk into the shop to look around, and the salesman says, "Here's the newest, lightest crank set. You'll drop 200 grams of weight with this thing. Take a look at these pedals—they're 165 grams lighter than yours." Really? And there is this guy dropping $300 on this stuff, and do you know what? He's twenty-five pounds overweight.

"Lay aside every weight and sin." It is easier said than done, right? Even the apostle Paul says, "I don't understand my actions. My intention is to serve God, to be faithful to God, but there's something in my life that keeps me from serving God, keeps me from doing God's will, keeps me from running the race, and I'm so messed up some times that I can't do the very thing I know I need to do."

And I know what he means. It's easier said than done. One writer recently put Paul's struggle in more contemporary terms:

> I'd like to have a cigarette tonight. Just one. Ten minutes of satisfaction, of letting my guard down, of doing whatever the heck I want to do at any particular moment. A cigarette tonight, a beer right now, and maybe I won't go jogging tomorrow. Shouldn't be that big a crisis, right?
>
> Except I quit smoking a month ago. For the second time in a year. And I *really* don't feel like quitting smoking all over again tomorrow…And if I let myself become a smoker again, I won't really enjoy any of the cigarettes I smoke. Very soon after that, I'll start feeling miserable…Because doing what I want to do makes me miserable. But *not* doing the things I want to do takes so much effort.[2]

Every sin, every hindrance, every weight that drags you down, lose it. But the flesh is weak, isn't it? That is why he throws out that word—*perseverance*. I wish there were a cleaner, more painless word than that. It sounds too much like work, like a lot of hard work that takes a long time. You might get through one week, but that is not perseverance. One lap around the track is not persevering. Not two laps, not four. This race is more like a marathon, right? That is what it is. And the author of Hebrews says you have to just stay in there, you have to stay in the game. And that is the radical word that separates weekend warriors from the genuine article when it comes to faith. Christians persevere. In a culture in which our choices are made on feelings, that is a hard word. You can get around the track once or twice on feelings, but those feelings wear thin the longer you're in the race.

A man says, "I don't want to be married to you anymore. You don't make me happy. I don't feel like I did when we first got married." I have done close to two hundred weddings now. Not once do I remember anyone ever vowing to stay together until the feeling goes away. That is just not part of the contract.

Perseverance is finding a way beyond your feelings in order to do what must be done. It is staying in the race even when it hurts, even when you do not have all the answers. And it is what distinguishes the genuine articles of this world from the weekend warriors.

A few years back I found myself torn over an issue in the church that seems to be dividing churches right and left these days. It is an issue that, for some, can only be resolved by reading selected passages from the Bible, especially the Old Testament; for others, it's an issue resolved only by practicing the uncompromising and indiscriminate love of Jesus. One particular family in the church was alone in their choice of the former method of resolving the issue, and the prospect of losing them became a growing concern for me. They called one afternoon to set an appointment with me to discuss their options, and I spent the next three days praying for peace, and grace, and understanding. I'm embarrassed to say that I also found myself reaching for whatever armor I could find, preparing for a painful confrontation, drawing a line in the sand and rereading every Bible passage I could find on the issue, which turned out to be a brief exercise.

On the afternoon of our scheduled appointment, I waited, and prayed, and contemplated the seemingly inevitable outcome. At three o'clock they walked into my office—she carrying a five-gallon bucket of water; he, a small hand towel. Before I could rise from my chair, she knelt down on both knees, and removing my shoes and socks, washed my feet in the warm, fragrant water—first the right foot, then the left, slowly, generously, with great care. He followed with the towel, quietly drying both heels and all ten toes, one at a time. Then, rising to their feet, they turned for the door without saying a single word. When I saw them sitting in the second row of the sanctuary the following Sunday morning, and every Sunday morning thereafter, I caught a glimpse of the grace and courage that perseverance requires.

I do not know if there is any other way to get around that track and persevere together, to endure the stuff that every one of us has to endure in our lives and in our church—the hardships, the disappointments, the sin that clings to us, the obstacles in our way, the misunderstandings and disagreements and imperfections—I do not know how to persevere in the face of all that without, as the author of Hebrews says, "looking to Jesus the pioneer and perfecter of our faith."

"Looking to Jesus," says the author of Hebrews. What does that mean? It means following the leader, the one who has already blazed the trail for us. It means doing what he did: the one who never untied his shoes and stepped out of the race; the one who stayed in the game. Just watch him, just follow him, and you will get around that track.

I want you to hear that. He doesn't say, "Look to Moses, or Abraham, or Sarah, or Rahab, or Martin Luther King Jr., or Mother Teresa, or SpongeBob SquarePants." He says, "Look to Jesus. Do what he did, and you'll get around that track."

And right there in the courtyard, Peter said, "Jesus? No, I don't know anyone named Jesus. Never heard of him." Three times. "No, Jesus who?" Three times. But look at Jesus, right there on the beach, after the resurrection. "Peter, it's me, Jesus. You do remember me, right? Do you love me?" Three times. "Do you love me? Then feed my sheep." That is a love that perseveres. Jesus had it.

"Look to Jesus," says the author of Hebrews. Look at him there in Pilate's headquarters, down there in Jerusalem, standing before Pilate, dressed in rags and bound in shackles, his head hanging on his shoulders. Pilate says, "Who are you, Jesus? You want me to set you free? You want all of this to go away? You want to step out of the race? I can set you free if you want. You don't have to do this." But Jesus said not a word. No way. He's in the race for the long haul. "I'm already free," he finally told Pilate. "Look to Jesus," says the author of Hebrews, "the pioneer and perfecter of our faith."

Look to Jesus, right there in the Garden of Gethsemane, where he's praying on the last night of his life. The disciples are right there with him. "We're with you Jesus, we'll stick with you till the very end." And minutes later they're sleeping; his best friends are lights out on the last night of his life, unable to carry his burden. It had to be heartbreaking for Jesus, but look at him. Before the sun would set the following day, there he is, hanging from a tree, whispering, "Father, forgive them, because they don't know what they're doing."

Look to Jesus, who never untied his shoes, never stepped out of the race; who persevered for our sake and for the sake of the kingdom of God. Jesus had game. Keep your eyes on Jesus. Do what he did.

As we remember the saints today, we're remembering those who not only persevered in their lives, but who fill the seats of the stadium right now and surround us with their faith and hope and witness, so that we will persevere in our own lives, and together as one body. If you listen carefully you will hear them cheering you on, pulling for you. *Stay in the race. Do not give up.*

Maybe your legs are weak, and your lungs are burning, and your heart is pounding, and you're out of breath. And maybe you just don't feel like running anymore. But they are on their feet, every one of them, because they know what's on the other side of the finish line, and they know what it's like to run this race.

Go the distance. Stay in the game. Don't bonk. Set aside every weight, keep your eyes on Jesus, and run with perseverance the race that is before you.

Video Clip Suggestion

Finding Forrester (Columbia Tristar, 2000)

When Jamal takes Forrester to Yankee Stadium, they walk out onto the field after the game, where Forrester tells Jamal the story of his brother's death, for which Forrester feels some responsibility. The death of his brother became a defining event in Forrester's life, which derailed his brilliant writing career and drove him into seclusion.

The preacher may choose to use this clip to illustrate how the pain and regret of our pasts become obstacles in our own journeys, and prevent us from getting around the track (1:25:00—1:30:00).

One Life to Give

Mark 12:38–44

He sat down opposite the treasury, and watched the crowd putting money into the treasury. Many rich people put in large sums. A poor widow came and put in two small copper coins, which are worth a penny. Then he called his disciples and said to them, "Truly I tell you, this poor widow has put in more than all those who are contributing to the treasury. For all of them contributed out of their abundance; but she out of her poverty has put in everything she had, all she had to live on." (Mk. 12:41–44)

I want you to think for a moment about your wallets. Most of you here this morning brought your wallets with you. If you didn't, let me remind you that I think it's a good idea to bring your wallets to church with you.

Think about your wallets for a moment. I don't want you to pull them out. I just want you to think about what's inside that wallet. Not the credit cards, not the driver's license, not the family photos. I want you to think about how much cash you have in your wallets. Some of you carry a lot of cash around with you; some of you travel a little light and swipe one of those cards wherever you go. But think for a moment: Off the top of your head, how much cash is in your wallet right now? forty dollars? twelve dollars? Twenty-two dollars and maybe a little change tucked in your pocket or rattling around at the bottom of your purse? Think for a moment about how much cash you have on you right now. And imagine just for a moment that whatever you have on you right now is all you have to your good name. No bank accounts, no credit or debit cards, no IRAs or CDs or fixed assets to cash in later. Whatever cash you have on you is all that you have left. When it's gone, it's gone. There's no more.

Now, I want you to think about this one question this morning: If what cash you have on you is all the money you have left in this world, what would you do with it? How would you spend it? How would you use it? If you have no one else to worry about—no kids to feed, no spouse to share it with, no outstanding IOUs; it's just you and your cash—what would you do with it?

I've got eight dollars on me right now. With eight dollars I could buy a Venti Vanilla Latte and blueberry scone. Maybe you have a little more than that on you today. What would you do with that? Would you splurge and buy a case of Slim Jims? Would you buy a one-way ticket on Southwest and fly to Vegas and put the rest on the blackjack table? Would you fill your car up with gas, or buy a handful of Lotto tickets? Would you go to the 99 cent store and stretch every last cent? What would you do with what you have?

There's a lot you might do with that cash. You could try to multiply it somehow, or you could just blow it and go out with a bang, or you could keep it for as long as you could and not spend a penny until the growl in your belly convinced you otherwise. There's so much you could do, but I'll bet my last eight dollars that you wouldn't do one thing with it: I'd bet my last eight dollars you wouldn't give it away.

Who would? Who would possibly be so foolish that they would give away every last cent they had? Once it's gone, it's gone. There's no more. You'd be a fool, right? That's your money. You need that money. You can't live without that money.

And a widow walks into the temple, walks right up to the treasury. Stands in line between Donald Trump and the silvery haired charlatan televangelist—the rich people, the so-called righteous people, the people who give big and give publicly and get all the recognition. She's a have-not in the midst of those who have everything and more. And you look at her curled up fingers and see her gripping her last two coins—that's all she has left; when it's gone, it's gone for good. And she's waiting in line, head bowed, eyes closed, waiting. Those warm, moist coins clutched in the shallow palm of her tired hand. Watch her.

Jesus says to his disciples, "Hey, come here and check this out. Take a good long look." And we say, "You've got to be kidding. She's not going to do what we think she's going to do. She's not going to give her last two coins away, is she?" And Jesus says, "Watch her. Just watch what she does." And we watch as she steps forward and raises her frail hand over the treasury bucket—the offering plate of the temple—and we watch her as she breathes deep and lets go of those coins. They fall through the air and barely make a clink as they land, but you can hear her breathe a sigh of relief as she lets go. It is the breath of a free woman.

I don't pretend to understand why Jesus wanted us to watch her. Most of us would agree that she is hardly the model for sound money management. She was poor going into the temple; and she was flat broke leaving it. She gave her last penny to a religious institution that Jesus himself said was spiritually bankrupt. Her meager offering wouldn't make a bit of difference to the bottom line of the temple budget. On the surface, it seems about as tragic as an elderly shut-in watching the television at midnight, picking up the telephone to give away her life savings to a sleazy televangelist wearing an Armani suit and diamond-studded gold rings.

And Jesus says, "Did you see that? Did you see what she just did?"

I don't know—from where I stand in this world, I have to confess that I just don't understand her. Her life story is so far from my life story that I do not understand what she is doing. Now, I used to think that I was more like her than the rest of those characters in the temple. There was a time in my life, going through seminary, when Lori and I were flat broke and pinched every last penny; but those days are behind us now. We've got a little more now than just a few loose coins. I'm not like her because I am not poor, and I have never once in my life given away my last two coins.

But I've never thought that I'm like the rich people in the story, either. I certainly don't feel rich. I don't live an extravagant lifestyle. I don't have everything I want. I still get nervous at the end of the month. I still hold my breath through those last few days of the month until payday. I'm not a rich man.

So I've always convinced myself that I'm somewhere in the middle—not poor, but certainly not rich, either. I'm right there in the middle, between the haves and the have-nots. I've never given away my last two cents, and I've never been able to give big like a rich man and still have enough at the end of the month. I'm not like either of these.

So help me out here—how do I use this passage to preach about giving? I felt trapped all week by this passage. That's what happens to you when you follow the lectionary—you have to preach the hard stuff. Some of you might think that the mother church tells me what I'm supposed to preach, but that doesn't happen. They just say, here's the scripture, figure out what it means, and preach it.

But there's no clean way through this one. I'll tell you why. If I told you today that Jesus wants you to give every last penny to the church, it wouldn't matter if you were as rich as Bill Gates or as poor as a cart-pusher on Skid Row—if I told you that, you'd never come back again. I'd be preaching to an empty church next week. And if I told you the flip side of that—if I told you that it didn't matter what you gave to the church, just give whatever you want, whenever you want to, like the rich people in the story; come and go, leave a little here and a little there, and that's just fine—if I told you that, we'd probably have a full house next week, but we wouldn't have a house, would we? No music, no Sunday school, no money for missions or youth programs or the poor. Well, that won't work.

There's just no clean way through this passage, because I know the minute I talk about giving in the church, you're already puckering up, and you say, "Here we go again. This is the problem with churches, they always want your money."

So I want to tell you about what this passage does to me, personally. I want to tell you what I have learned this week. I took a long, hard look at my life, and I learned that I am closer to the rich people in this story than I am to the poor widow. The story is told for this very purpose – to remind me that I am not poor, but far more rich than I care to admit. Jesus says, "Watch that woman." He says that because I am one of the rich people in the story, and she has something to teach me.

I want to come clean now. I am rich. I make $60,000 a year, and that fact alone puts me in the wealthiest 10 percent of the world's population. I have a home that is now worth far more than I paid for it, and I will pay it off in twenty-five years. I have a retirement fund that will carry Lori and me in our old age. Most months I have just enough left over to catch a Dodger game or take Lori out to a nice restaurant. I am not poor. I am rich.

I still wake up at night sometimes and wonder how in the world I'm going to put my three kids through college on $60,000 a year. I still wonder if my retirement fund will be enough to buy a new set of teeth when I need them. I still don't know how I'm going to pay for braces for the kids, or get the credit card balance down, or buy a new set of tires for the minivan. But I'm not worried about it, really. I'm not down to my last two coins. There are ways to manage when you are rich like me.

But I will tell you a secret about being rich. It can be a burden. When I was flat broke years ago I could breathe deeper, like that poor widow in the story. I worried less about my money back then. But now that I am rich, I find that it is harder to pry those coins loose from my hands, and I do not feel so free. That is why, I believe, the church does a stewardship campaign every year—to remind me to give generously, sacrificially; to teach a rich man how to be a free man.[1] You cannot read the Bible truthfully and convince yourself that you do not have enough. You cannot read it and still say, "I'd like to give more if I could." When you look at those people in the book of Acts who gave everything away for the common good, so that no one had need, you see an image of a people who were free, and that is what I want for myself.

So I've made up my mind about this. I will give until I feel good about what I give, until my giving proves to myself that spiritual things are more valuable than material things and that you cannot serve both at once. I will not hold back like those other rich people in the story. I will not give a little here and a little there, whenever I feel like it, in order to be noticed. I'm just going to give because I know that God knows my heart and sees in secret what the world cannot see. God knows whether I am free or not. And if I give like that, I know that my giving will make a difference in my life and in this church and in this world.

The more I understand this, the more free I am. Like that widow in the temple, who breathes a sigh of relief when she drops her last two coins in the treasury, there are moments when I, too, can do that. I'm not there yet. But like Jules Winnfield says in *Pulp Fiction*,

"I'm trying real hard, Ringo." I'm trying, and it's working. I'm giving, and I'm breathing. But it's hard.

I pulled into the gas station last week, got out of the car, and a woman in her mid-twenties approached me. A real pretty woman, by the way. I think that was part of the plan. She said, "Excuse me, Sir, do you have a couple of dollars so I can buy some gas and get home?" Now, I'm not a sucker for this stuff. I don't care what the story is; I will give people what I can when they ask for it. I give it not because I'm a sucker, but because I believe in Jesus, and Jesus says, he who welcomes another with a gallon of gas in my name welcomes me, so there you have it.

I give her a few bucks. And then I start filling up the tank, and I watch her go inside the mini mart. A couple of minutes later, she comes out with a pack of cigarettes and a diet soda. She smiles, waves, and I breathe. I just let it go, and breathe.

I can't change the world. I can't buy another person's freedom with my money. But I know one thing. I know that when I give it away, I'm buying my own freedom, I'm changing myself, I'm making a difference in my own life, I'm exercising my own freedom.

So here we are at the end of the year, and we have to do a stewardship campaign. We have programs to pay for, buildings, staff, missions, and this is how we do it every year. I asked the landscapers, when they put in all the trees for this new building—I asked them to plant a money tree. But apparently that didn't happen. So we have to do this stewardship campaign.

And everyone holds their breath because no one wants to hear about money and no one wants to preach about it. So I said I'm not going to preach about your money. I'm going to preach about your life—your rich, comfortable, faithful, free life. I'm not going to ask you, "How much are you going to give," I'm going to ask you, "How free are you?"

And then I'm going to let you figure out the rest, because if there is one thing this story from Mark tells me, it is this—no one is watching. Whether you're rich or poor, no one is watching—no one, that is, except Jesus. People say, "What I give to the church is between me and God." And I agree. That's what the story says. It says, Jesus is watching.

That's all I wanted you to know this morning. Not one of us here today is poor. We are all of us very rich, and Jesus is watching us, wondering what we will do, waiting for us to cast our vote for freedom.

Video Clip Suggestion

Phenomenon (Touchstone Pictures, 1996)

(to illustrate that the things to which we give ourselves are the things we tend to love most)

While the guys at the bar try to convince each other that George was not really special after all, Doc tells Baines a secret about George— he bought his lady's chairs, and that's why his lady is sticking with him. "Every woman has her chairs, something she needs to put herself into, Baines. You ever figure out what Lisa's chairs were, and buy them?" (1:39:00—1:41:00).

Get Up and Walk

John 5:1–9

When Jesus saw him lying there and knew that he had been there a long time, he said to him, "Do you want to be made well?" (Jn. 5:6)

He came into my office with fire in his eyes and the sour smell of bourbon and sweat on sweat—a nameless man with track marks up and down both arms and hands that trembled for a fix. "I'm hungry," he said frantically. "I need some money. I need you to help me." I sat quietly as he reached into his bag of stories—stories of children he hasn't seen and jobs he couldn't hold and friends who've betrayed him and strangers who've robbed him and on and on—you know the story. "But the church is supposed to help people like me; you must do something; I need some money, I need, I need, I need…" I tried to tell him that I couldn't give him what he thought he needed, that I could only help him find a rehab to sober up and heal, that I would do this if he really wanted to be helped, that I knew where he could go, but he was already gone before I could finish, scurrying off into the hot, dry desert of addiction like a thirsty man craving salt.

She came to me one day looking for relief, for answers, for anything that would staunch the pain and burden of her life. A million-dollar home, three kids, a rock the size of Gibraltar on her left hand, a lifestyle that would make even Robin Leach blush, and—yes, and this was the problem—a husband 3,000 miles away with a woman half his age. Thirteen years of marriage undone in a heartbeat, and with it went the lifestyle, the comforts, the pride, her identity. I prayed with her; I encouraged her to come to church, to lean on God and community and the love of strangers here who would support her and walk with her through the valley of the shadow. But she left that afternoon, and I've wondered ever since what else she might have come looking for.

The kids have this hamster at home. I can hear it spinning on the wheel every night, all night, trying to get somewhere. It just runs and runs to nowhere. The kids left the cage door open one day this week. It's the door to freedom, right? It's the Red Sea parted, for heaven's sake. We looked all day for that hamster. Turned the whole house upside down. The hamster is gone, we said. Free at last. Then the tears, and the heartbreak, the grieving. We were just about ready to light the candle and begin the memorial service for the hamster when, later that day, just as the sun went down, I could hear the faint sound of that little wheel spinning. The hamster had returned to Egypt. Came back from the promised land, all the way back to Pharaoh. Couldn't live without that wheel.

Desire can be a powerful force in our lives, a lure for better or for worse. It can lead us out of where we do not want to be anymore, or it can be so seductive, so addictive, that it keeps us stuck in the very place we do not want to be. Bruce Springsteen was right—"everybody's got a hungry heart."[1] But it is not the hunger that will either sink us or save us; it is what we seek to satisfy it.

Matthew is almost three weeks old now. He desires one thing at this age—just one thing. Lori's got it; I, on the other hand, am anatomically hampered in this department. He knows what he wants, knows what he needs. And he knows where to go to get it. I can appreciate that single-mindedness, that clarity of focus, that undistracted mission of his. But I know something about Matthew, because it is true of all of us. The older we get, the more we can lose that focus. We forget where to look for that spiritual milk, and we will chase after so many imitations, so many illusions, so much junk food—power, wealth, unhealthy relationships, addictions, status, and public image…you fill in the blank. Hamster wheels.

Desire can become a dangerous enemy or a best friend. I think of Augustine, who in the fourth century made memoir an art form with his book *Confessions*. You look at the top-ten best-sellers list these days, and 75 percent of those books are memoirs, right? Augustine was one of the first to start this trend. His *Confessions* is required reading at many colleges. It is a book about desire, really. Augustine was a world-class party animal in his day. He tried it all. He was a lost, wandering soul. He looked for salvation in philosophy, in material wealth, in knowledge, in the pleasures of the flesh. You name it, Augustine tried it. He would come so close to claiming Jesus Christ for himself, then his desires for other things would get the best of him, and he would wander off again and again. It is a heartbreaking story most of the way, because he knows what he *should* desire, but he cannot bring himself to that commitment. Halfway through the book he writes the words that I want you to hear today, because it just about says it all about the conflict of desire that we all go through. He writes:

> When at last I cling to you with all my being, for me there will be no more sorrow, no more toil. Then at last I shall be alive with true life, for my life will be filled by you. You raise up and sustain all those whose lives are filled by you, but my life is not yet filled by you and I am a burden to myself.[2]

What do we desire in our lives? What are we filling our lives with these days?

Jesus shows up one day at the pool of Bethsaida and asks a certain man that question. This man had been crippled for 38 years, and he's been showing up there every day because he wants to be healed. His religion had set up a way to accomplish that healing. The way it worked at the pool was simple—a variation on the "last one in is a rotten egg" theme, except in this case, everyone was a rotten egg except the *first* one in. People with all kinds of illnesses, some more trivial than others, would gather around the pool and wait. They would wait for the water to be stirred up, apparently by some angelic presence, as tradition would have it, and the first one to jump in got the healing. Now, this was good news if you had a hang-nail or heartburn, but if you were paralyzed you were fresh out of luck, right? So this man had a better chance of climbing Mt. Everest in this case, because he could not jump in the pool on his own, and worse, there was no one willing to throw him in.

But Jesus drops by the pool one day and sees all these swimmers in Speedos™ and goggles taking their marks on the blocks, right? And he sees this man lying there and he says to him, "So, you want to be made well?" Jesus had a sense of humor, didn't he? What does he expect the man to say? "No, Jesus, I'm actually here for the tan and the strawberry daiquiri." "Of course that's what I'm here for," the man says. But it's a good question, don't you think? Do you really want to be made well? Is that really your *desire*, or is this just a game you play so that everyone thinks that is what you want? If Jesus showed up to church some Sunday morning, I think he would ask the same question. Do you want to be made well, or is this just a *thing* you do? Whatever baggage you brought in here this morning, do you really want to let it go, do you really want to get up and walk, or would that be too much for you?

One of our members here has been in Alcoholics Anonymous for almost eight years now. He has sponsored a lot of recovering alcoholics during that time. He told me not long ago that he's chased a few pretenders away over the last few years. He's said to them, "You don't really want this, you're not ready for this, you're just playing the game. So go back out there and drink some more. Live it up. Do whatever you have to do to wreck your life big-time, then come back and talk to me." He really means that. He knows that unless a person wants to be healed, unless that is his heart's desire, he will never find it here. That is good theology.

So Jesus, convinced that the man really desired healing in his life, said to him, "You don't need this pool to be made well. Get up, and walk." And that is what the good man did.

Jesus said it was that simple, and that was not the only time he said it. "Ask, and it will be given you; search, and you will find; knock, and the door will be opened for you" (Mt. 7:7; Lk. 11:9). You remember that, right? Jesus was saying that if you desire the right things, the things that God desires for you, then ask for them. He was not talking about stuff; wasn't talking about a new SUV or hair for your widow's peak or a run on the stock market or a miraculous healing at the revival. He was talking about himself, his strength, his presence, his life in your life. He was talking about the things that matter to him. Seek first the kingdom of God, and all the rest of what really matters will be given to you.

Jesus never said that if you want it bad enough you'll get it. He said if you seek it hard enough, you'll find it. And there is a difference between the two. We are not short on wants in this world. We want our kids to succeed and find happiness and grow in love and grace, but there are a million other wants that get in our way each day.

I coached my son Casey's baseball team this year. Thirteen kids on my team. And do you know something? There were parents of kids on my team that I never once met the entire season. Drop them off, pick them up. Drop them off, pick them up—for four months. There were parents that sent their nanny to watch their kid play games. To love your child, to grow him in grace, you've got to get up and walk.

If you want it, seek it. We want to make a difference in the world, want to make a different world in our own little corners of the world, but there are a million other distractions that get in the way, right? I talk with people who say they would like to do something in the church—serve in some way, do something meaningful, something more fulfilling than the rat race. Maybe join a small group, do a mission trip, teach Sunday school. "So why don't you?" I ask. "Why don't you do it right now?" "*Can't*," they say. "I just can't make that commitment yet. I'm too busy. Nine to five, the golf game, bunko night, and weekend getaways." Sometimes that hamster wheel is not slavery, but self-indulgence, which is a very real form of slavery. I know what Jesus would say. If you want it, then get up and walk. Otherwise, get used to the poolside view.

What do you want to do with your life? What are you seeking, and how many hamster wheels are getting in the way of that? Get up and walk, says Jesus. Obey your thirst, your passions, your holy dreams. There is so much more than the hamster wheels. The cage door is wide open in your life. What is it that you desire, that you cannot live without? Get up and walk and seek it out.

In his autobiography of illness and triumph, Lance Armstrong writes, "While I was sick, I told myself I'd never cuss again, never drink another beer, never lose my temper again. I was going to be the greatest and the most clean-living guy you could hope to meet. But," he writes, "life goes on. Things change, intentions get lost. You have another beer. You say another cussword. How do you slip back into the ordinary world? That was the problem confronting me after cancer."[3]

Lance Armstrong almost didn't make it back, even after he defeated cancer. His first comeback was a failure. He gave up. He didn't have it anymore; he wasn't the same. His bike gathered dust. He says, "I was a bum. I played golf everyday, I water-skied, I drank beer, and I lay on the sofa and channel-surfed." Finally, his fiancée laid it all on the line. She said, "You need to decide something. You need to decide if you are going to retire for real, and be a golf-playing, beer-drinking, Mexican-food-eating slob…I just need to know so I can get myself together and go back to work to support your golfing. Just tell me."[4]

Do you really want to be made well? Sometimes we need people in our lives to put it straight like that, to test our desires, to jam up our hamster wheels long enough for us to see the truth, to challenge us to overcome the obstacles and move forward. Get up and walk, or get used to the view.

Video Clip Suggestion

About Schmidt (New Line Cinema, 2002)

Sitting atop his Winnebago, Warren Schmidt stares at the star-lit sky and talks to his dead wife, Helen, asking her for forgiveness for not being the kind of husband he could have been, and granting her forgiveness for her affair with Ray. This clip marks a major turning point in Schmidt's life as he leaves behind his self-pity and resolves to face a future of acceptance and empowerment (1:13:00—1:15:00).

PART 4

Reconciliation

They were five complete strangers, high school students with seemingly nothing in common, forced to spend a Saturday together in detention: a brain, a beauty, a jock, a rebel, and a recluse. Before the day was over, they broke the rules, bared their souls, and connected with each other in a way they never dreamed possible. In 1985 *The Breakfast Club* became an emblematic film for an entire generation, laying bare the struggles of family brokenness, teenage sex, peer pressure, and hurtful stereotypes, and exposing our growing sense of alienation from each other, from ourselves, and from those in positions of authority.

> **Brian:** Dear Mr. Vernon...We accept the fact that we had to sacrifice a whole Saturday in detention for whatever it was that we did wrong, what we did was wrong. But we think you're crazy to make us write this essay telling you who we think we are. What do you care? You see us as you want to see us...in the simplest terms and the most convenient definitions. You see us as a brain, an athlete, a basket case, a princess, and a criminal. Correct? That's the way we saw each other at seven o'clock this morning. We were brainwashed.[1]

In a culture that prizes social categories, individualism, competition, sexism, stereotypes, and widespread alienation, the church is called to an alternative consciousness that makes reconciliation with neighbor, with self, and with God our highest priority and the litmus test of our confession. Taking our cue from a God who, from the beginning of time, has sought to reconcile us to himself, and having been given a new commandment by Jesus to *love one another as I have loved you*, Christians are obligated to take the initiative in demonstrable acts of neighborliness and reconciliation in the world.

The sermons in this unit call the reader to a reconciled life, claiming repentance as the first step toward reconciliation with God; daring us to see, like Bartimaeus, the real brokenness and alienation in the world that we both fear and ignore; standing with Mary to announce the coming age when those who are alienated will be lifted up as instruments of God's reconciliation with the world; and finally, hearing the voice of God, claiming us as God's beloved, in whom God is pleased.

Road Work Ahead

Luke 3:1–6

"'Prepare the way of the Lord,
  make his paths straight.
Every valley shall be filled,
  and every mountain and hill shall be made low,
and the crooked shall be made straight,
  and the rough ways made smooth;
and all flesh shall see the salvation of God.'"
                                    (Lk. 3:4b–6)

Some people just tell it like it is. Have you ever known someone like that—someone who just cuts to the chase and tells you the honest truth, even when it is the hard truth, the one truth you need to hear? Those people are rare, aren't they? No beating around the bush; no smoke-screening; it is what it is, take it or leave it.

My son climbs right up on my lap and gives me a bear hug, looks me in the eye deeply and says, "Dad, you've got a big belly." Thanks for that, buddy, now why don't you just go on out and play in traffic, okay? I used to come home on a Sunday afternoon, after a long morning of preaching two services—after preaching a sermon that I just knew was *the* sermon, so well-crafted, so deeply insightful and imaginative and moving, right? I'd come home and ask Lori, "So, what did you think of the sermon?" I used to do that. I've learned not to do that anymore. "You really want to know?" she'd say, which was more of a statement than a question, really. On some Sundays she'd say, "Well, now, you tried real hard, didn't you?"

Some people just tell it like it is. But those people are rare, because those people often have nothing to lose, and people who have nothing to lose in this world are very rare. Doctors tell it like it is, but that's what we pay them to do. "How much time do I have left?" you ask. And they just tell you what they think—"Six months, maybe." Collection agencies tell it like it is, but that's because the only thing they have to lose is what you already owe them—"Pay the balance, or pay the piper." Nothing to lose there.

But they are rare, those truth-tellers. And it has been that way since the days of the Old Testament prophets, whose sole purpose was to tell the truth on God's behalf, and who were feared because of it. Isaiah was one of them. To the people of Israel he said, "Ah, you who call evil good / and good evil, / who put darkness for light / and light for darkness, / who put bitter for sweet / and sweet for bitter… / who acquit the guilty for a bribe / and deprive the innocent of their rights!" (Isa. 5:20–23). Woe to you. Repent while there is still time.

Jeremiah stood up in church one day—interrupted the preacher—and announced, "Scoundrels are found among my people… / they have become great and rich, / they have grown fat and sleek. / They know no limits in deeds of wickedness; / they do not judge with justice / the cause of the orphan, to make it prosper, / and they do not defend the rights of the needy" (Jer. 5:26–28). The Lord will judge a nation such as this. Return to the Lord, while there is still time."

There is nothing like a truth-teller in church to wreck a Sunday morning, right? It makes the coffee and donut after church stick in your throat, doesn't it? That kind of thing gets old real fast, which is why there was a period in Israel's history when the prophets were silenced. That period lasted four hundred years. Four hundred years, and not a single prophet to stand up and tell the truth about God when it needed to be told. Four hundred years, and not a prophetic word from God was ever uttered. That is a long time to just let things run their course. That is a long time to let the inmates run the asylum. Truth-tellers were not just rare back then. They were extinct, and you can imagine that the people in high places of power liked to keep it that way.

But Luke says, "Hold on now, I think I hear something—an echo, the thundering of a single voice bouncing off the walls of the desert canyons just east of Jerusalem—out there where the Jordan River cuts through the distant landscape of sand and rocks and silence. It is the echo of a single voice, uttering a single word that, if you strain to hear it—if you listen real hard—sounds a lot like the word, '*Prepare.*' Listen to that. I think that's what is being said. '*Prepare. Prepare the way of the Lord.*' It's been four hundred years since we've heard a word like that. Prepare the way of the Lord. That is no ordinary voice; no ordinary message; no ordinary messenger."

And Luke says the people went out to the wilderness in droves just to hear the messenger: Baptists and Methodists and Lutherans; rich people and poor people; priests and poets and politicians; addicts and convicts and soccer moms and MBAs. They all went out there to hear something—to hear something that they had not heard for four hundred years, but longed to hear every waking moment of their lives. They went to hear that God was about to do a new thing. They went to hear that there was more to this life than the life they were living. They went to hear that there was another way to God, a way that did not require them to crawl through that endless, complicated, exhausting maze called religion, which always seemed to send them in circles in their search for the Big Cheese, and which often left them starving at the end of the day.

Some people just tell it like it is, and John the Baptist was one of them. They went out to hear him preach because they knew that John had nothing to lose, and people who have nothing to lose by speaking the truth are completely free to speak it, and completely free to allow you to accept it or reject it. They knew that John was not on the temple payroll. He was not a sell-out to lobbyists down at the State Capitol. He did not have a job to protect, or a career path to jeopardize, or a retirement plan to pad. John was free of all that. He was free to speak the truth, and it was the truth that led them out to hear him.

I have never met a soul so free. The people who steal the spotlight these days are rarely so free. Preachers, politicians, C.E.O.s, talk-show hosts—look real close and you will almost always see a string or two attached, a hidden agenda, a conflict of interest. From Rome to Wall Street to Washington to Times Square, it is hard these days to distinguish between truth and fiction, between the straight-talker and the charlatan, between the word we *need* to hear and the word we *want* to hear.

That is why John the Baptist went to the wilderness, and that is why the people went to hear him. He went there unfettered by the world and the world's demands, so that he could speak the truth, so that the truth could be heard. And the people were so hungry for the truth that they took no offense at his message: *Prepare the way of the Lord. Repent. Make the highway of God straight in your life, so that God can find a way in.* It was the best sermon they had ever heard.

Why? Because it was so simple and true, that sermon, that they could actually understand it. "Every valley in your life," said John, "raise it up. Did you dig yourself a hole, get yourself in a tough spot? Then get out the earthmover and fill it in. Whatever it takes, fill it in. Every mountain in your life, every obstacle, every wall and speed bump, get out the earthmover and level every last one of them. Is something getting in the way of God in your life? Move it. Every little crooked way in your life, straighten it out. Every bad habit, every hurtful pattern in your life, every wrong you call right, knock it off. Every rough edge—the words, the attitudes, the way you react to people—smooth it out." That makes perfect sense, doesn't it? John was a straight-talker. No three points and a poem. Just one big point, made clean and simple: Do some road work. Build a highway in your life, an inroad, so that God can find a way to you.

And I will tell you something—something very strange about that sermon. It wasn't religious at all. John wasn't trying to get us to join a church or learn a creed or pay our temple tax or barbecue a goat for an offering to God. That wasn't John's thing. John understood that you can be religious and still be a mess; he knew that religion was often an excuse for avoiding God altogether. Instead of telling us to become more religious, John called us simply to become more honest about ourselves—to survey the landscape of our souls to see if there is any way in us that is not of God; to turn over the soil, remove the rocks, knock down the detours, open up the dead-ends, and build a straight way for the One who is coming.

John knew that things in our lives are not as they should be, not as they could be. Some of us are a mess; some of us clean up better than others. But there are parts of our lives that, if given the opportunity, we'd like to go back and fix, go back and do all over again, the right way. We ask, *How did it come to this? How did I get like this?* Whether it is the wars we wage with ourselves or with our families or with our neighbors or with countries half a world away, John says, "If you want to get to Bethlehem, you've got some changes to make. And you can do it now."

"It's too bad what's happened in Iraq. We should just nuke that whole country and get it over with. It's a lost cause over there" someone says. I know what John would say. The road to Bethlehem goes right through Baghdad. People, get ready for the one who comes to hammer swords into plowshares, the Prince of Peace.

I saw the woman on the 405 Freeway this week, her hand waving that ever so subtle gesture at a truck that cut in front of her. I watched as the finger went up from the front seat of her beamer. On the back of that beamer, the license plate frame read: "Got Jesus?" John says, "To get to Bethlehem, take the 405 north. People, get ready."

I heard the man barking orders in the garden center of the Home Depot. "Get me six bags of mulch, five flats of ground cover—hurry up, I don't have all day." The man was about thirty-five years old, ordering an old, worn-out Hispanic man more than twice his age. I watched him as he struggled to lift the bags onto the cart under the angry, arrogant eye of the white man. "People, get ready," says John. "The One who comes is not only a Savior, he is a Judge, bearing an axe that will strike at the very root of the tree."

At my daughter's swim meet this week a six-year-old swam the wrong stroke in his heat. Everyone else was swimming breaststroke, but this kid was swimming freestyle. And the father raged, and he swore, and he shouted to get his boy to stop. But the boy could not hear him and kept swimming, and the father stormed the pool deck in fury, pulling his howling boy out of the water by the arm, and I heard John all the way from the Jordan, proclaiming a baptism of repentance for the forgiveness of sins.

These are just a few of the people I passed by on my way out to see John this week, and for a moment I thought I was looking pretty good, comparatively speaking. I tried to convince John that I was not one of them, that a few small repairs would do just fine, that the inroads of my life were still in pretty good shape.

But before I could explain, I saw behind me the dark shadow of the wrecking ball looming on the horizon, and felt the terrifying rumble of the bulldozer drawing near, and heard that razing voice crying out in the wilderness the truth that only a free man can speak—"Prepare a highway for the Lord; make his paths straight."

Video Clip Suggestions

O Brother, Where Art Thou? (Touchstone Pictures, 2000)

Delmar is baptized in the lake while his two partners look on. Upon coming out of the water, he declares, "Well, that's it, bugs, I been redeemed! The preacher warshed away all my sins and transgression. It's the straight-and-narrow from here on out, and heaven everlasting's my reward!" Everett says, "Delmar, what the hell are you talking about? We got bigger fish to fry." Delmar replies, "Preacher said my sins are warshed away including that Piggly Wiggly I knocked over in Beaufort" (DVD, chapter 4).

The Emperor's Club (Universal Pictures, 2002)

Mr. Hundert gives Sedgwick "one last lecture," saying that "all of us, at some point, are forced to look at ourselves in the mirror and see who we really are," and when that moment comes for Sedgwick, Hundert says, it will be a painful revelation. Sedgwick replies that he will do whatever he needs to do to get what he wants, whether it's "lying or cheating or whatever," and that he'll worry about his contribution to the world later. As Sedgwick argues his case for a life without principle and integrity, he is unaware that his son is in the room, listening (1:33:00–1:36:00).

About Schmidt (New Line Cinema, 2002)

(to illustrate the difficulty of smoothing the rough places of our lives and removing the mountains and valleys that separate us from others)
Warren Schmidt decides to patch things up with his old friend Ray, from whom he became estranged after discovering Ray had an affair with Warren's wife, who is now dead. While on his road trip, Warren stops at a phone booth and calls Ray. After pouring out his heart, he discovers that he's been talking to a message machine, and he deletes the message and hangs up (1:10:00—1:12:00).

Bruce Almighty (Universal Pictures, 2003)

(to illustrate that sometimes people just do not make a bit of sense)
Equipped with the mighty power of God, Bruce gets his revenge on the news reporter who beat him out of the coveted anchor position; he scrambles the news anchor's speech on live TV (DVD, chapter 11).

Vision Quest

Mark 10:46–52

Immediately he regained his sight and followed him on the way. (Mk. 10:52b)

So we had that sound up in the attic this week. You know what sound I'm talking about, right? That covert chewing sound, right above the ceiling in the master bedroom, directly above the bed. Lori hasn't slept a wink in three days. That sound—teeth on plywood, chewing like a beaver; chewing through Lord knows what, nonstop. I didn't know there was that much wood up in the attic; never knew what was up there until this week. The little feet with long toenails scratching and scurrying back and forth, back and forth. Lori slept on the couch. There was no way she was sleeping with that sound above her. I tried to convince her that I couldn't hear it, so she brought a group of neighbors through one afternoon. Some of them said it was a rodent; some argued that it sounded more like a grizzly bear. Lori suggested that it was Mike Tyson, chewing away the wood like Evander's ear lobe.

She finally sent me up there. Have you ever had that experience? Get the ladder, climb up all five steps; you stop at the top, staring at that little two-by-two square of drywall attic lid. You reach up to move it, and you can hear the little feet right above you, scampering around. It sounds like a whole army of them up there. I reach up to move that little lid, and I just know that this is something I should not be doing. I think to myself, *Feldman, do you really want to know what's up there? Do you really want to see what's behind that door? What are you going to do about what you will see when you poke your head into the darkness, when you see that part of life that is better left unexposed?"*

We go through life with a sense of relief that there are things we don't have to see in this world. Just pretend it's not there, right? Out of sight, out of mind. The stuff we can't explain, the stuff that scares us, the stuff that goes on in the world, in our lives, in our relationships, that we do not see; we know it's there, but as long as we don't see it, it doesn't exist, and we don't have to deal with it. But sometimes it comes so close that we can hear it, feel it, and we know that it does exist, that it is real, that there is a part of life that we have to deal with, despite not knowing if we are even remotely prepared to face it.

The story today is from the gospel of Mark, about a blind man named Bartimaeus, who wants nothing else but to be able to see the world as it really is, to be delivered from his personal darkness and to see the world with all its color and texture and height and depth. But does he really know what he's asking for? Because to see the beauty of life, to see the color and feel the texture, means also to know the horrible horrors and dark terrors of life, the stuff that is not so beautiful, the stuff that very few sighted people choose to see. Does he really want to see the kind of world he's been living in? Does Bartimaeus really want to see the kind of world that is going to do terrible things to the one who restores his sight?

It's early morning in Jericho. You are one of the twelve walking the streets with Jesus. You're drinking a double shot Venti Latte because you didn't sleep a wink last night. You were tossing and turning all night long, because you are only a single day's journey from Jerusalem. And just last night, before you all went to bed, Jesus told you, for the third time, what was going to happen down in Jerusalem. He said, "When we get to Jerusalem, I am going to be arrested and condemned to death. I will be mocked, and spit upon, and flogged, and killed. And after three days, I will rise again." You all just sat there, stunned, shocked. Then, just like that, he turned off the lights, and said, "Good night. Sleep tight." But nobody slept last night. Nobody said a word.

So there you are, the following morning, walking behind Jesus, sipping your latte, trying to keep up with Jesus as he leads the pack through downtown Jericho. It's a mess downtown: people everywhere, half of whom are following you, trying their best to get a piece of Jesus. And out of the chaos, there's a blind beggar over on the sidewalk, shoulders slumped, neck arched, skin on bones, calling out to Jesus,

"Jesus, Son of David, have mercy on me!" Everyone's trying to get him to shut up, but the harder they try, the louder he cries out. "Jesus, Son of David, have mercy on me!" It's such an embarrassing thing for everyone. Most beggars in Jericho follow the standard, city-approved, tourist-friendly method of just holding up a sign and keeping their mouths closed, but Bartimaeus is shameless, and he won't shut up. Bartimaeus is making a scene.

So Jesus stops in the middle of the road, looks over at you and says, "Go get him." You do as the master says. You walk the old blind man over to Jesus, and turn his shoulders slightly, until his weather-beaten face is set directly on Jesus. And Jesus asks him straight up, "What do you want me to do for you?"

Now I want you to hear that question, because it's not a trivial question; it's a particular question that requires a particular answer. Jesus asks the question because he wants to find out what Bartimaeus believes is possible for Jesus to do. Do you want a hot meal? I can do that for you. Do you want a hotel room for the night, a warm bath, and HBO? I can arrange for that. I think Jesus asks that question because he knows that most people would prefer a handout over a healing.

I see a dozen people a month walk off the street and into my office. They all have stories to tell of hardship, job loss, foreclosure, illness. Some of their stories are true, some of them are not, though most of the time I try not to make such judgments. I listen for as long as I am able, at which time I ask, in some form, the same question Jesus asks Bartimaeus. "What do you want me to do for you?" In ten years of ministry not one has ever asked me to try to heal them. Not one has ever asked for spiritual counsel, or prayer, or a support group. I know, I know—no amount of prayer seems to quiet the thunder of a hungry belly or pay the electric bill. But it is true, as Jesus once said, that some of our personal demons in this life are driven out only by prayer.

Bartimaeus doesn't have a great life as a blind man, but his begging bowl gets him three square meals a day; all he has to do is sit there and beg, and people give. No nine to five at the office; no bills to pay; no annual reviews; no fears of layoffs. What do you want, Bart? Do you want a handout? But Bartimaeus asks for the one thing that only Jesus can give, which is why Bartimaeus is an extraordinary example of what it means to believe in Jesus Christ. "My teacher," he says, "let me see again." It's a request that would change his life. No more begging bowls; no more sitting on the corner; no more turning a blind eye to the hard stuff of life out there in the world. And Jesus says, "Go; your faith has made you well."

What Bartimaeus asks for, and what he gets, has to be one of the most terrifying gifts that anyone could possibly receive. You wouldn't think so, given the fact that all of us here have grown up with sight and have been sensitized to all that we see in this world. But we are adaptable creatures. We have acquired the gift of selective blindness. We tune out and turn away from what we don't want to see—the stuff we don't understand, the stuff that scares us, the stuff that hurts just looking at it, the stuff that doesn't fit into our systems of faith.

In my first year of seminary I boarded a bus along with all the other first-year seminarians and traveled to downtown Los Angeles. I'd been to L.A. a million times before, but not to this part of L.A. We made three stops. The first was to Union Rescue Mission on Skid Row. As we pulled in, hundreds of people lined the streets—people in cardboard boxes; people with old shopping carts filled with rags, aluminum cans, plastic bottles; people with children; people with addictions; people with nowhere to go—all standing outside of the Mission, waiting for a hot meal. As we walked inside the mission, dressed in our polo shirts and brand-name pleated slacks and skirts, we were out of place. A man with burning red eyes and fury in his voice put his finger in my chest and said, "What are you looking at, fool?" That was the PG version of what he said anyway. It was the first time in my life I had seen human suffering on such a large scale.

From there we walked to a building where migrant women sat behind sewing machines for ten hours a day. Some of them, I am sure, are still there today. They do not earn a wage that will pay the rent, or feed their hungry children, or buy them a way out. Some of them, the noncompliant, outspoken ones, work only for two weeks; instead of receiving their first check on payday, they are turned over to the INS for deportation. That's how the garment industry keeps its costs down.

From there we walked a few blocks to a building that shelters runaway teens caught in the deadly web of prostitution—most of whom are under the age of fifteen, many of whom are HIV positive. There are more than 200,000 of these children nationwide. I had never before met one of them.

It is the part of life I have chosen not to see. It is the horrifying stuff of life that I do not understand. But more than that, it is the kind of stuff that turns my faith upside down and inside out, because I fear that so much of what I have called faith is not faith at all, but a fantasy that only makes sense insofar as I do not see the nightmares of those whose lives are far different from mine. It's easy to believe in a God who is good when the life you have is not all that bad to begin with. Give God a nickel, and you get back a dime. That works for most of us. But what happens when you're out of change, when the begging bowl is empty?

Bartimaeus chose to see that kind of world. I know it doesn't say that in the text, at least not directly. But read between the lines. Jesus tells Bart that his faith has made him well, but I believe the real measure of how well his faith really is lies in what he does with it once he gets his sight back. Did you hear this part of the story? Bartimaeus followed Jesus. I mean he really followed Jesus, with his two feet. And not just anywhere; not just around town, not just for the day. Mark says he followed Jesus, joined the team, stuck with Jesus all the way into Jerusalem, where the cross was already being prepared. Bartimaeus didn't have to do that. He could have just gone to church from there, paid his tithe, and joined the Building Committee. He could have decided that his newfound sight was a blessing, but I think he understood that it was a burden, too.

I imagine that, just after his healing, he walked side by side with Jesus through town. I imagine that he asked Jesus where he was going, and I imagine that Jesus told him the same thing he told his disciples on three separate occasions. "I'm going to Jerusalem to be arrested, beaten, mocked, humiliated, and killed." I trust they had that conversation. And Mark says, "Bartimaeus followed Jesus."

I want to have that kind of faith—the kind of faith that is unafraid to see everything, the good and the not-so-good, the beauty and the terror of life, the light and the darkness. I want that kind of faith because I know that unless my faith is tested by the darkness of the world, the light that I see will not make my faith well. If I cannot believe in the darkness what I know to be true in the light, then my words, my deeds, my convictions are worth nothing more than the stuff that fills begging bowls. They will feed me for a day, but come nightfall, I have nothing for tomorrow.

Anne Lamott wrote a book several years ago about what it's like to be a writer, and how writing is a metaphor for life. Toward the end of the book, she wrote these words, which are as much about the life of faith as they are about the life of writing. She says:

> We write to expose the unexposed. If there is one door to the castle you have been told not to go through, you must. Otherwise, you'll just be rearranging furniture in rooms you've already been in. Most human beings are dedicated to keeping that one door shut. But the writer's job is to see what's behind that door, to see the bleak unspeakable stuff, and to turn the unspeakable into words—not just into any words but if we can, into rhythm and blues.[1]

If you were to peek behind that one door and see the bleak unspeakable stuff—in your own personal lives, in your families, in your relationships, in your world—would your faith be so true and honest and humble that what you spoke in those places could be heard as rhythm and blues, and not as a noisy gong or a clanging symbol? What word of faith and hope could you offer that would be as true in the darkness of the world as it is in the light?

I talked with a pastor a few weeks ago. After fifteen years of local church ministry he accepted a chaplaincy position in a children's hospital. He told me how it changed his faith. He said, "I realized that most of what I preached on Sunday mornings in church doesn't preach in a place where life hangs in the balance every day. You learn to choose your words more carefully in a place like that. You learn to be more honest."

So I want to send you out with a mission this week. Take it or leave it; it's up to you. I want you to peek behind one of those doors in the castle that the world prefers to keep closed. I want you, like Bartimaeus, to follow Jesus down to Jerusalem, all the way.

Visit a convalescent home this week. Just walk through the halls if that is all you can bring yourself to do. See a kind of suffering and loneliness that perhaps you haven't seen, and think of an honest word of hope that would be true in that place. What could you say about Jesus in a place like that?

Spend some time at a soup kitchen, or a food bank, or a homeless shelter. See something that looks entirely different from the world you know, and think of a word of hope, of love, of faith that would ring true in that place.

Spend some time with someone who suffers from a mental illness, or a physical illness, or a terminal illness, or a deep spiritual loneliness—what could you say that wouldn't be begging bowl fodder?

I know it sounds like too much to ask. There is precious little time in our lives for anything more than the begging bowls we all of us need to fill in order to get by. There's the nine to five job, and the kids to bathe and feed, and the bills to pay, and the dishes to put away—all before the sun goes down on another day of work. But so much of what we do in a single day of work we tend to do with our eyes closed and with a faith that is not so well, and someday someone with an empty stomach and fire in his eyes and fury in his voice may very well put a finger in your chest and ask you—"What are you looking at?" And if your faith has made you well, as it made Bartimaeus well, maybe, just maybe, you'll have wisdom enough to say, "Jesus. I'm looking right at you, and what I see is Jesus."

Trading Places

Luke 1:47–55

"He has brought down the powerful from their thrones, / and lifted up the lowly." (Lk. 1:52)

So did you hear about the kidnapping of Santa a couple of years ago? That's right, according to *Reuters News Service*, Santa Claus was kidnapped just before Christmas 2002 in Ontario, Canada. Here's the initial report of the incident:

> Canadian thieves calling themselves *Grinch Enterprises* kidnapped a Santa Claus figure off an Ontario family's front lawn and are holding the jolly icon for ransom, the owner said on Wednesday.
>
> The group—which has struck at the same family home before and demanded a similar ransom—wants the owners to collect canned goods for a food bank in return for getting their plywood Santa back before Christmas Day. "My reindeers are still there, but Santa Claus is gone," the owner told reporters.
>
> The group has left several ransom notes where the four-foot tall Santa once stood. Some of the notes contain instructions; some of them include photographs of the missing Santa. "In the one I just got last night," said the owner, "Santa's in front of the Sarnia General Hospital, which probably means that he will be injured quite soon if I don't meet their demands."

The owner, Evelyn Hussey, said she plans to ask local schools to help collect about 700 cans of food. "I want my Santa back because it looks ugly outside without him. I just want him back."[1] Grinch Enterprises is on to something, if you ask me. They've got a Christian vision of Christmas that is infused with holy defiance. Grinch Enterprises knows one thing that God wants us to understand this Christmas: *The poor matter.* And like Grinch Enterprises, God goes to great lengths to make that clear. The poor matter to God, more than they matter to the world.

While we're busy this Christmas making a list and checking it twice, baking fruitcakes and buying gifts for all the fruitcakes in our lives, we read a gospel story today that reminds us that Christmas was, from the very beginning, born on the hopes and faith of the poor. It is a story about God looking down on all creation and choosing to use the poor as the primary instruments by which to reconcile God to the world. Of all the people whom God could have chosen for this purpose, God chose the poor.

God didn't exactly follow the conventional wisdom of the day. Had God hired a marketing firm from Madison Avenue to get the message to the world, the gospel story of Christmas would look like a Gap™ commercial, right? Young, middle-class, professional-looking twenty-somethings dressed in turtlenecks and black denim jeans, dancing to Supertramp and posing with a purpose. That would have made a statement about who God is and what God's up to at Christmas. Or they might have produced a commercial with God behind the wheel of a brand new beamer, or appearing on CNBC ringing the closing bell on Wall Street. That would have made a statement about what God was up to in the world. It would have put God right in the spotlight.

But God, of course, chose another, more humble, way. God looked down from heaven and made the conscious choice to be born into this world in the life and hope and faith of the poor, who no one noticed, who no one would ever believe. I don't believe that was an accident. I don't believe God chose the first Joe and Mary God happened upon. I believe God knew what God was doing.

The powerful? No, that won't work—they'll just use me to advance their own causes and agendas. The wealthy? No, I'd just get lost in all their stuff. The famous? No, they hate to share the spotlight, and the press loves to scandalize them. The poor? Yeah, that'll work. The poor. They still have enough room in their lives to receive me. The poor have nothing to get in the way.

Oscar Romero, the great contemporary martyr, once said that "No one can celebrate a genuine Christmas without being truly poor,"[2] and as hard as it is to admit it, I believe he's right, because it is the poor of this world who, having little or nothing material to give, know well what it means to receive unconditionally.

It's not so with you and me. Christmas, for us, is a season of giving, and so much of our giving so often has strings attached to it. We give reciprocally. We give, so often, because someone is planning on giving to us. And if they do give to us, and we have nothing to give in return, we feel like they've one-upped us, right? We feel like they out-did us, that we owe them something, that we're somehow indebted to them. When someone gives us something, we have to pay attention to them, right? Giving has a way of saying to the receiver, "I matter. Listen to me." Giving is an expression of power in this world.

I think God knew that. God knew that to use the powerful to bear the Holy into the world, we'd all try to return the favor somehow, try to balance the books. But, of course, this is one gift you can't match. God knew that. So God decided to play musical chairs with the powerful and the poor, and when the music stopped at Christmas, the poor were given the only remaining seats, and the powerful just stood there, wondering what happened.

Mary was one of those who got it all started. I want you to look at Mary, because God chose Mary—and chose her not in spite of, but because of, her "low estate." We don't talk much about that in church. We clean Mary up at Christmas. We paste her white, creamy, middle-class face on Christmas cards every year, right? You look at those cards and Mary looks like a thirty-year-old South Orange County soccer mom in a SUV, right? She's beautiful, so full of potential and opportunity and success—a stay-at-home mom with a M.B.A. The church, over the years, cleaned her up in order to make her more presentable, worthy, believable—in order to make her look just like us.

But Luke says she was a peasant from Judea, or Tijuana; maybe she lived in her car in South Central L.A.; or in a shelter in Santa

Ana. She was a face in the crowd; a statistic; a drain on the tax payers; an unskilled, uneducated, unemployed, illiterate maiden who stood out on the corner with all the *jornalleros* looking for a day job, and most often went home empty-handed. You can't put that on a Christmas card, but that's who she was. A faceless, nameless, forgotten nobody who's now pregnant with a child—the father of whom no one can really agree on.

God chose Mary and thought she had all the right stuff to bear God's only son into this world. Throwing on flesh and blood to become human was God's last remaining option for saving the world, and God found Mary, of all people, to be the best possible candidate to carry out the plan. Of all the people God could have chosen, God chose Mary—worthless to the world, but treasured by God.

Christmas is God's divine protest against the powers of this world, which have proclaimed that you have to be *someone* in order to make God's list; that you have to satisfy certain worldly criteria in order to make a difference in this world. Christmas is God's judgment on that kind of world. Christmas is God's proclamation that the poor are treasured. Christmas announces a new age in which, as Mary sings, the proud are scattered in the imagination of their hearts, the mighty are pulled from their thrones; those of low degree are exalted, and the hungry are filled with good things.

Mary is saying that the world has now been turned upside down, that a new age is dawning, that the kingdom of God is breaking in, and the King is on his way. Those who previously had no place at the banquet table are now given the place of honor. Those who once had nothing to give to this world are now pregnant with the hope of a new world.

And she bears a son who confirms it. What is his first sermon, according to Luke? Jesus stands in the synagogue, unrolls the scroll of Isaiah, and what does he preach? "The spirit of the Lord is upon me, to preach good news to the poor, to proclaim release to the captives, recovery of sight to the blind; to set at liberty those who are oppressed. And to announce that a new day, a new age, has dawned."

The divine plan that grows in the womb of Mary is about to change the world. The poor, at last, will be lifted up by God, and given the keys to the kingdom of God. The powerful and the poor will trade places in God's eyes. And the Christmas hope is that they will trade places in our own eyes—that we will look at the faces of the poor and see what God sees: not someone who is worthy once a year of our seasonal generosity, but someone who is worthy of our very best love; someone who gave birth to Jesus; someone Jesus chose to live with, and die for. They are the ones who maintain our lawns and clean our homes; their backs are raised to the sky in the strawberry fields; they stand on busy corners waiting for work; they line the halls of nursing homes like old, abandoned cars. You don't have to look very far to find Mary in this world.

These are the people God chose to use to reconcile the world to God, knowing that they possessed a hunger for a new world altogether; that while the powerful seek to hold on to the world order they have worked so hard to create, the poor seek a whole new world altogether—a world built not on power and might and wealth, but a world built on the redemptive mercy of God.

In John Steinbeck's *The Grapes of Wrath*, after the Joads lose their farm in Oklahoma to the devastating dust storms and the heartless machine of corporate banking, they head west with hopes of work and new life. Their journey is a slow, progressive tragedy of loss and hopelessness. Every opportunity fails them; starvation and illness circle overhead like vultures at every moment; work eludes them; hope wanes.

Near the conclusion of the novel, the boxcar that has served as their temporary home is flooded by the engorged rivers during a violent rain storm, sweeping away their last, meager possessions, including the tired jalopy that brought them west. During the storm, as the waters rise up in the boxcar, Rose of Sharon, the young, optimistic daughter, gives birth to a stillborn child. Her very name is symbolic; the early church referred to Jesus as the Rose of Sharon, the beautiful symbol of love that rises up out of the low plains of eastern Palestine. Steinbeck makes this connection in the closing pages of his novel. Rose of Sharon, in the midst of her tragic, aching experience becomes the Christ-bearer to a sick, starving man. As the Joad family flees the violent flood, they take shelter in an old barn, encountering two dark figures huddled in the gloom—a man who lay on his back, and a boy sitting beside him, his eyes wide, staring at the newcomers. Pointing to the man on the ground, Ma Joad asks the boy,

"What's the matter'th that fella?"

The boy spoke in a croaking monotone. "Fust he was sick—but now he's starvin'."

"What?"

"Starvin'. Got sick in the cotton. He ain't et for six days."

Ma walked to the corner and looked down at the man. He was about fifty, his whiskery face gaunt, and his open eyes were vague and staring…"Your pa?" Ma asked.

"Yeah! Says he wasn' hungry, or he jus' et. Give me the food. Now he's too weak. Can't hardly move.… Got to have soup or milk. You folks got money to git milk?"

Ma said, "Hush. Don' worry. We'll figger somepin out."

Ma looked at Rose of Sharon huddled in the comforter. Ma's eyes passed Rose of Sharon's eyes, and then came back to them. And the two women looked deep into each other. The girl's breath came short and gasping.

She said, "Yes."

Ma smiled. "I knowed you would. I knowed!"

Rose of Sharon whispered, "will—will you all—go out?" The rain whisked lightly on the roof.

Rose of Sharon hoisted her tired body up and drew the comfort around her. She moved slowly to the corner and stood looking down at the wasted face, into the wide, frightened eyes. Then slowly she lay down beside him. He shook his head slowly from side to side. Rose of Sharon loosened one side of the blanket and bared her breast. "You got to," she said. She squirmed closer and pulled his head close. "There!" she said. "There." Her hand moved behind his head and supported it. Her fingers moved gently in his hair. She looked up and across the barn, and her lips came together and smiled mysteriously."[3]

It is Mary, if you ask me, given the one task she alone can do, giving the one gift she alone can give, holding the world in her arms, bringing Christ to the world.

Video Clip Suggestion

Unstrung Heroes (Hollywood Pictures, 1995)

(to illustrate the hidden value of the lost and forgotten things of the world)
In this touching film, Franz Lidz, a young Jewish boy, comes to depend on his two absurdly quirky uncles for comic relief and life lessons while dealing with his mother's grave illness and death. In this scene, Franz joins his eccentric uncle in search of lost things in the city. As his uncle rescues lost balls from the city's gutters, he tells Franz that he "can hear the sounds of the children who played with them" (0:52:48—0:54:52).

Signed, Sealed, Delivered

Mark 1:9–13

And a voice came from heaven, "You are my Son, the Beloved; with you I am well pleased." (Mk. 1:11)

I was twenty-three years old when the bishop laid his hand on my head and ordained me deacon in the United Methodist Church. I stepped onto the stage at the annual conference, knelt down on both knees, bowed my head, and held my breath. It was the culmination of a long spiritual journey, and I expected it to be filled with drama and emotion and the awe of being added to the ranks of an apostolic succession that spanned back in time for two thousand years.

I expected my heart to skip a beat at that moment. I had hoped that I might have some vision of seraphim descending upon me, or that I might glow, or even hear the very voice of God speak to me in some dramatic way. What I got instead was the hand of my bishop laid upon my head before a crowd of two thousand people and the words, "*Take thou authority to preach the word of God in the church of God.*" It was simple, quick, and to the point. No visions. No drama. Just a hand on the head and a few words, and that was it.

I had expected so much more, but when I opened my eyes, I felt no different. No rush of blood to the head; no knee knocking; no deep spiritual epiphany that would change my life in an instant. I was the same person, only now I had been given the keys to an office that I suddenly felt completely unprepared to enter—to preach the word of God, to baptize, to care for the dying, to bury the dead; to balance a budget, and counsel the lost and brokenhearted, and maintain the peace on the church softball team. What I thought would be a blessing turned out to be an incredible responsibility for which I felt totally unprepared, despite the certificate of ordination on the office wall that said otherwise.

I stumbled and fumbled for months that first year as a pastor. There were days I didn't know whether to pick my head or scratch my nose. I had stars in my eyes in those early days of ministry, and spent most of my time chasing my tail, learning the ropes, and trying not to fail. Then I got the call that Bryan had been admitted to the hospital. Bryan was eighty years old, a lifelong Methodist, dying from emphysema, and he called the office to ask if I would visit him in the hospital before he ran out of breath.

I sat with him that day, next to his bed and the machines and the *Do Not Resuscitate* sign on the wall. I didn't know what to say or do, and I think that's why Bryan asked me to come. He wanted to teach me what I needed to learn: the art of presence, the ministry of care that goes beyond words or deeds, the ministry of being there when no words or deeds will do. He wanted to teach me how to be a pastor, and, having known and supported me for two years, he took it upon himself to do so. We talked, we prayed, we talked about his funeral—the hymns, the scriptures, the prayers. Bryan was the teacher; I was the apprentice. And when the lesson was over, and I turned to head for the door, Bryan spoke the words that became for me the words of my real ordination. Bryan grabbed my hand, drew a slow, wispy breath, and said, "I love you."

That was the day I became a pastor. The day Bryan Robinson said, "I love you," it was as if the seraphim had descended from heaven, and the voice of God had truly spoken; the lump in the throat was real, and for the first time in my early life as a minister, I trusted that, despite all my inexperience and fears, I was blessed to do the work I had been called to do in this world.

We all need those moments in our lives, don't we? Those moments when we are named, when we are given an identity that transcends our abilities, and transcends our illusions and our shortcomings, too—when we are known not by our deeds or our jobs or the false images of how we would like to be perceived in this world; when we are loved simply, and completely, with a kind of love that makes us more than we are.

We can go through an entire lifetime and never know who we really are—mostly, I suppose, because we often spend our lives trying to become who we are not and never will be. *Who am I*, we ask ourselves? And the world is so accommodating, isn't it? If we do not know who we are, the world will surely tell us. We are too short, too dumpy, too bald, too lumpy, too small and too flabby and too flat and too fat. We are always one product away from being just right. We live in a world of purchase, where we can buy our identities to match the projection of what the world deems lovable and acceptable.

And if that does not work, we can find our name in the things that we do—our jobs, our roles, our careers, our degrees, and our titles. We define ourselves by what we do. We are regional sales managers, or elementary school teachers, or ordained ministers, or administrators—all titles that point to the work we do that defines who we are in this world. It is easy to confuse making a living with making a life, isn't it? The average gainfully employed American puts in something like 52 hours a week at work. Now I want you to think about this. That is at least half of your waking life. But then there is the commuting time, the overtime, the prep time off the clock, the phone calls and the e-mails and voice mails, and it is clear that the majority of our time is spent making a living, which has a way of making our lives. So much of our identity is drawn from our work: The fruits of our labors, the results, the bottom line all have a way of validating our existences. Lose your job, and it feels like a little death, doesn't it? When the kids leave home, and the nest is empty, you grieve the loss of them, and of yourself. Who am I going to be now?

Do you remember reading *Death of a Salesman* back in high school? Willy Loman is obsessed by his dreams of being a big-shot, a money-maker, a player in this world. Even into his sixties, he's striving for a life he will never live, exaggerating his successes, covering up his failure and lies and infidelity, and everyone knows it but Willy Loman. When the truth finally dawns in his life, it is too much for him to bear. Standing at his father's grave, his son Biff says, "He had the wrong dreams. He never knew who he was."[1]

But to be named by something beyond our dreams, beyond the expectations others have of us; to be given a name that transcends even our successes and our roles and titles and our good looks and six-pack abs; now this is what we yearn for above all else—to be named by a love that loves completely, and to be content with that.

It is what even Jesus needed, this naming. And that is why he needed to be baptized, I believe. He steps into the Jordan, and John baptizes him. And as he comes up out of the water, the heavens are torn apart and the Spirit descends upon him like a dove, and a voice from heaven—God's voice—says, "*You are my Son, the Beloved; with you I am well pleased.*"

It is the first time we see Jesus as an adult in Mark's gospel. He is about thirty years old, and he is ready now to step out onto the world scene. Mark says Jesus hasn't taken the job of Messiah yet. No healings, no miracles, no speeches or successes or crowds yet. Before he takes the job, God gives him his name. Not Healer, or Prophet, or Messiah, or Preacher, or Rabbi—not a name based on what he does or will do or should do; but a name based on how God sees him. His name is Beloved. "You are my Son, and before you do anything, before anyone tells you what they think of you, I'm telling you what I think of you. I'm telling you you're wonderful, you're beloved. I'm telling you I find great pleasure in you."

It was something he had to go through before he could do the work that he was created to do. It was his defining moment. Whatever he would do with the rest of his life would be marked by that moment, that naming. He would know who he was. He was given a name, not according to what he had done, not according to his plans or his hopes or his dreams, but according to his relationship with his Father in heaven. The rest of his life would be an exercise in remembering that name—wherever he was, whatever he did, it would either fulfill that name or betray it.

And Mark says his test came soon enough. Before anyone had a chance to question his identity, or critique it or challenge it, Mark says that the Spirit immediately drove him out into the wilderness to think about it. Forty days of no work. Forty days of no one telling him who he was or who he should be or who they needed him to be. Except one, of course. Mark says his name is Satan.

Unlike Matthew and Luke, Mark doesn't say much about the temptation of Jesus, only that he *was* tempted, and the angels attended to him. But we all know what temptation is like, and we can assume that it was no different for Jesus. *You are not enough. You can become something more. You are not who you think you are. You do not have to settle for what you have become.* When the pipe is passed on the school yard, when you tip the bottle dry at midnight, when the attractive bombshell at the office tells you things your spouse didn't think to tell you, when the pot of gold is left unguarded, these are not only opportunities to deceive others about our true identities; they are the occasions by which we first deceive ourselves.

The truth of our character is always measured by our ability to cling to our identity in Christ in moments of temptation—an identity pronounced at our baptism and sealed irrevocably by the Holy Spirit. And the biblical understanding of the role of Satan is that he is to broadside us in those moments by slandering that identity. Satan is the great *accuser*, according to Christian tradition—the one who will try to tell you who you are, who you are not, what is wrong with you, who you will never be. Satan is the great *slanderer*. In the wilderness, in the raw, lonely moments of temptation, his mission is to steal your identity, to tempt you away from it, to try to give you a different name, to tell you that you are not who you thought you were, and never will be. His mission is to strip you of your memory as God's beloved sons and daughters.

I do not know what you believe about Satan. Maybe you think he is real in this world; maybe you are more comfortable talking about evil in more general terms and not personifying it. I do not think it matters if you believe one way or another. But you cannot get around the fact that we are tempted every day; every day, we encounter a new test, a unique and often unforeseen challenge to our identities in Christ. Will we break? Will we pass the test? Will we remember who we are as children of God, or will we forget? Will we allow our identity, our name in Christ, to be slandered? or will we live up to our name as a Christian, as a beloved child of God?

Sometimes the temptation is to become more than we know we are. Sometimes it is to become less. How many times have you said, or heard someone say, after blowing it big-time, after really messing up, "I'm only human."? Have you ever heard that? "Hey, I failed; I really messed up, made a bad choice, crossed a line. But what do you expect? I'm only human, right?"

Those who have been baptized in Christ cannot get off so easily. In our baptism, as in the baptism of Jesus, you are no longer *only human*. You are a new creation. You might still be messed up. You might still mess up. But in Christ you are no longer only human. You are beloved. You are changed. How did Jesus survive for forty days in the wilderness? Because he knew that he was more than "only human." He was God's beloved. He was changed forever. There was no going back.

We lose that memory. It is so easy to lose that name—"Beloved." We are like the people referred to in the letter of James, who hear the word of God, who see the face of the beloved staring back at them in the mirror, but who, upon going away, immediately forget what they look like.

There is a theory in the field of psychology called *cognitive dissonance*. It acknowledges that for all of us, there is a gap between our ideals and our actions, our goals and our deeds, between the image that we have of ourselves and the image that we want to project to other people. *Cognitive dissonance*, occurs when the story we tell about ourselves is not an accurate portrayal of who we really are.

Standing in the middle of that gap, trying to hold those two poles together, can be a painful and exhausting experience, and is the cause of much of our sin. We pretend to be innocent when we are guilty; we pretend to have it all together when we are falling apart at the seams; we pretend to be strong when we are most vulnerable; we pretend to be successful when we have failed miserably. We try to be what others expect of us and we cannot measure up. It is the gap between where we are and where we think we are, and it can keep us in the wilderness for a lifetime.

But there is a faithful alternative to that tension, and in his letter to the Philippians the apostle Paul calls that "contentment." I know who I am, he says. My citizenship is in heaven, and my life, my name, is in Christ. Because of that, I have learned to be content with whatever I have, and I am able to do all things through him who strengthens me.

Richard Selzer is a former surgeon and distinguished writer who, in 1991, was diagnosed with Legionnaire's Disease. In his memoir of his brush with death and his painful journey to life, he recounts an experience in which he had collapsed in his hospital room in a failed attempt to escape the terrors of hallucination and delirium that had plagued him for ten successive nights. He feared that his mattress was scheming to devour him alive, and he resolved to flee. He made it to the sink, and saw his reflection in the mirror. What he saw was not a man, he writes, but a specter, an image of madness—mouth agape and huffing, the whites of his eyes visible around the pupils. Sliding to the floor, he cried for help into the empty darkness of the room, soiling himself from head to toe.

Then the nurse walks into his room and clicks on the light. "That was a stupid and dangerous thing to do," the nurse says. "Just look at ye, sprawled." He hands Selzer his oxygen mask, coaches his breathing, and holds his hand.

> "I'm your solution," says the nurse.
> "What?"
> "I'm goin' to solve ye. Trow ye into the toob, that's what."
> "The toob?"
> "Aye, the toob."
> He kneels over and scoops Selzer into his arms, carries him to the bathtub, and peels off the soiled raiment. He draws the bath, lowers him in. "It's like dippin' a sheep. To get rid of the bugs…"

Speaking in the third person, as if watching it all from a distance, Selzer writes,

> "With soap and washcloth, he bathes the man, then scoops water…and pours it over his head, again and again. Now he rubs lather into the man's scalp, massaging, rinsing."
> "Ah, just wait till I get t'rough wit' ye…" From where he lies in the tub he can see reflected in the Irishman's face…the satisfaction the man draws from his work.
> And at last the man is lifted from the tub, clean, calm, and sane. Rubbed dry, he is carried back to his room.
> "Now how do you feel?"
> "Euphoric," he tells the nurse.
> "You what?"
> "*Phoric*. That means being carried. The *eu* stands for contented. I am happy to be carried." And he feels the heat

and the strength of the solid man infusing him, entering his veins; his breathing lightens, his brain clears…It is the true moment of cure."[2]

And from the waters of our own baptisms we are happy to be carried, too. The Spirit that descends upon us, naming and claiming us, is the same Spirit that carries us through the wilderness, through every dark night and every raw moment of temptation, reminding us who we are, calling us by name—"Beloved sons and daughters of God."

Video Clip Suggestions

Magnolia (New Line Cinema, 1999)

Bobby is a whiz kid on a network game show who has won a small fortune with his brilliant mind. His father rides his son's success all the way to the bank, until one day Bobby cracks on the show and loses. His father's disappointment breaks Bobby's heart. Later that night, he comes to his father, saying, "You need to be nicer to me." His father replies, "Go to bed…" (2:54:25—2:55:08).

About Schmidt (New Line Cinema, 2002)

Waking up on the roof of his Winnebago after a night in the "wilderness," Warren Schmidt wakes up "completely transformed," "a new man" who knows who he is, what he wants, and determined that nothing will ever stop him (1:15:00—1:16:00).

Notes

Part 1: Ambiguity

[1] Readers of Walter Brueggemann will recognize this assessment of the state of the church in postmodern, post-Christian culture. For more on this, see Brueggemann's *Deep Memory, Exuberant Hope: Contested Truth in a Post-Christian Culture* (Minneapolis: Augsburg Fortress Press, 2000).

As If It Were So

[1] While the person and event referred to here are indeed real in every way, I have, for obvious reasons, changed the person's name.
[2] John Wesley's letter to Wilberforce can be found in its entirety at the United Methodist General Board of Global Ministries Web site, which features a comprehensive online resource of Wesleyan history and theology (http://gbgm-umc.org/umw/wesley).

The Splintered Throne

[1] Fred Craddock's sermon, "Enduring the Small Stuff," in *Ten Great Preachers* (Grand Rapids: Baker Books, 200), 41-54, served as inspiration for this sermon. Although preaching on a different text, Craddock is helpful in reminding us that faithfulness does not come all at once, nor do most acts of faithfulness present themselves to us as big, dramatic events or opportunities. Rather than "writing one big check," as Craddock says, most of us will write a series of "smaller checks" over the course of our entire lives. I am indebted to Craddock for this insight, and note here his influence on this sermon.

The Journey of the Magi

[1] I am indebted to Walter Brueggemann for this insightful exegesis in *Inscribing the Text: Sermons and Prayers of Walter Brueggemann,* ed. Anna Carter Florence (Minneapolis: Fortress Press, 2004), 129–32.
[2] "Heaven," by Live, on the album *Birds of Prey* (Radioactive Records, 2003).

Every Here and Now

[1] "Numb," by U2, on the album *Pop* (Polygram International Music, 1997).
[2] Article about Warren Allen Smith, *Celebrities in Hell* (Fort Lee, N.J.: Barricade, 2002) in Christina Dalton, "When the Roll Is Called Down Yonder," *Los Angeles Times Magazine* (January 11, 2003): 8.
[3] As told to me by my friend and colleague, the Reverend William Johnson.

You Have No Idea

[1] See http://christianity.about.com/library/graphics/gruncru.jpg.

Part 2: Suffering

[1] Robert Ellsberg, ed., *Flannery O'Connor: Spiritual Writings* (New York: Orbis, 2003), 146.
[2] Ibid., 153.

All That You Can't Leave Behind

[1] See Annie Dillard, *For the Time Being* (New York: Alfred A. Knopf, 1999), 159.
[2] William Willimon, "Taking Up the Cross," *The Christian Century* (March 2, 1983) 173–74.

Blessed Thorns

[1] Flannery O'Connor, *Wise Blood* (New York: Farrar, Straus, and Giroux, 1967), 113
[2] Anne Lamott, "Falling Better." This article is found exclusively online at www.salon.com. A subscription to this Web site is required to view Lamott's articles.

The Big Reveal

[1] Cynthia Audet, "My Scar," *Utne* (May–June, 2003): 96.
[2] As quoted by Tom Beaudoin in *Virtual Faith: The Irreverent Spiritual Quest of Generation X* (San Francisco: Jossey-Bass, 1998), 99.
[3] Dave Eggers, *A Heartbreaking Work of Staggering Genius* (New York: Simon & Schuster, 2000), 207–8.

It Takes One to Know One

[1] "Taxi," *Heads and Tales* (Elektra, 1972).
[2] C. Douglas Weaver, *A Cloud of Witnesses: Sermon Illustrations and Devotionals from the Christian Heritage* (Macon: Smyth & Helwys, Inc., 1993), 157.

Part 3: Transformation

Home Alone

[1] Robin Williams, *Live on Broadway* (Sony Music, 2002).
[2] Jimi Izrael, "Rosa Parks," "History and Heroes." This article appeared online at www.africana.com.
[3] See Maxie Dunham, "Be More than You Are," in *Maxie's Perceptions*, an online archive of Dunham's brief reflections on faith, found at http://www.asburyseminary.edu/news/publications/perceptions/021097.shtml.

Keepers of the Flame

[1] Annie Dillard, *For the Time Being* (New York: Alfred A. Knopf, 1999), 153.
[2] "Another Day," in *Rent: Original Broadway Cast Recording* (Dreamworks, 1996). Words by Jonathan Larson.
[3] John Steinbeck, *The Grapes of Wrath* (New York: Penguin Putnam, 2002), 124.

Born to Run

[1] Thanks to Thomas Long for this image in *Hebrews* (Louisville: John Knox Press, 1997), 128.
[2] Henri Mazza, "Pulling Myself Together: Is your life like this, too?" *Utne* (May/June 2003): 94–95.

One Life to Give

[1] I am indebted to Fred Craddock for his sermon, "Old Story, New Ending (Luke 16:19-31) in *Overhearing the Gospel* (St. Louis: Chalice Press, 2002), 137–42, in which he points out the dangers of losing one's freedom as a "rich man."

Get Up and Walk

[1] "Hungry Heart," on *The River* (Sony, 1980).
[2] Augustine, *Confessions,* trans. R. S. Pine-Coffin (Baltimore: Penguin Books, 1961), 232.
[3] Lance Armstrong, *It's Not About the Bike: My Journey Back to Life* (New York: G. P. Putnam's Sons, 2000), 187–98.
[4] Ibid.

Part 4: Reconciliation

[1] *The Breakfast Club,* written and directed by John Hughes, distributed by Universal Pictures, 1985.

Vision Quest

[1] Anne Lamott, *Bird by Bird* (New York: Anchor Books, 1994), 198.

Trading Places

[1] This story originally appeared online via Reuters for *Yahoo! News* on December 19, 2002.
[2] Oscar Romero, *The Violence of Love* (Farmington, Pa.: The Bruderhof Foundation, 2003), 126.
[3] John Steinbeck, *The Grapes of Wrath* (New York: Penguin Putnam, 2002), 453–55.

Signed, Sealed, Delivered

[1] Arthur Miller, *Death of a Salesman* (New York: Penguin Books, 1976), 138.
[2] Richard Selzer, *Raising the Dead* (New York: Whittle Books, 1993), 88–93.